D1748324

"Helen's ability to learn and share her learnings is her superpower! She has taught me the importance of being able to think expansively while maintaining intimate connections. My first encounter with her over 10 years ago shifted how I saw networking and building relationships, which has had the most profound impact on my career. She is a master, and I know this book will help catapult your career and personal life as you learn to connect with others by networking from a truly authentic place."

- Dr. Vumile Msweli, CEO Hesed Consulting

"The thing that makes Helen Nicholson not just respected but loved by clients and delegates is that she walks her talk. Her advice is grounded not only in research but also in her own life experiences. She brings both to life in this book, one that offers an invaluable opportunity to those who will never get to hear one of her keynotes, or attend one of her workshops to absorb some of the wisdom she shares. And for those who have been lucky enough to hear her firsthand, this book will feel like she's right back in the room with you!"

- Niven Postma, Harvard Business Review contributor

"In today's fast-paced world, where genuine human connection is becoming increasingly crucial, there's a lot to discover. This book offers valuable insights from an expert in networking and building authentic human connections, making it a must-read for anyone looking to thrive in our modern world."

- John Sanei, Singularity Futurist

"I have learned a lot from listening to Helen present and teach us why networking is key, and now the book cements these tools in a highly practical way. The book is a must read. I have been using the tools she shares in this book and I've benefited enormously.

- *Hannah Sadiki, CEO Bidvest Financial Services*

"People are often surprised to hear that, as a professional speaker, I'm also an introvert. I'm a lot more afraid of the networking session than I am of delivering a keynote. This is why I found Helen's book so valuable. It has helped me close the gap between my on-stage performance and my off-stage networking in a way that feels a whole lot less intimidating, which has in turn won me more stages. Win! Highly recommended."

- *Rich Mulholland, International speaker and Founder of Missing Link*

"It was nearly two decades ago that Helen first encouraged me to turn being an introvert (and I am an off-the-scale introvert) into a superpower. She's finally put her wisdom and practical insights on paper. This book will change your life as you discover new and valuable insights into building your personal and professional network, even when your energy preference is to leave the room and spend more time with yourself. I cannot recommend this enough."

- *Dr Graeme Codrington, CEO, TomorrowToday Global*

"Networking for Introverts by Helen Nicholson is a timely book for a number of reasons. First, it's a real invitation to introverts to consider their gifts and strengths in a world where noise dominates and it's often hard for introverts to hear themselves think, and therefore the barrier to networking. I have often felt inept because my brain needs to ping around multiple files before I can offer meaningful input to conversations, and I feel 'slow'. This book has given me permission to slow things down so that I can bring myself to the party.

Secondly, I feel it's fair to say that even some extroverts and ambiverts have found connecting post-Covid tricky, as social muscles atrophied in the isolation. Helen's book helps to retrain those social muscles.

Thirdly, it's a bit of a smack on the head for those of us who believe our brand narrative will be accurately shaped by what we do, assuming people are paying attention. They're not, and so the importance of writing our own narratives as introverts becomes glaringly obvious and vital as you devour the insights and practical tips that Helen shares in this book.

I put the book down, and I was properly confronted by the fact that I've spent a good portion of my life building the brands of corporations but not enough deliberate time crafting and narrating my own. This was a big wake-up call for me, but now I know what to do after reading this book.

Mostly I love how Helen pays attention to helping the most reluctant of us to find our space in the world. So if that's your struggle, grab a copy of this insightful and compassionate guide."

- Wendy Nagel, Founder of The Potentiality Company

#1 BESTSELLING AUTHOR

NETWORKING
— FOR INTROVERTS —

HELEN NICHOLSON

tn co.
PUBLISHING

This book is dedicated to my two precious friends who died in 2023:

Merinda Davies - my mentor and my beloved Kelly girl boss
Antenocia Gitzner (Ants) - the bravest woman I knew!

Ants 50th Birthday, 2022

Sands, me and Merinds -
The Kelly Girls!

Scan the QR code below, and access all the additonal resources for this book.

Originally published in South Africa in 2024 by
TNCo Publishing, Johannesburg, Gauteng

Copyright © 2024 TNCo Publishing, Johannesburg, Gauteng.

The right of Helen Nicholson to be identified as the Author of the Work has been asserted by her in accordance with the Copyright Act 98 of 1978.

All rights reserved. No part of this publication may be reproduced, stored in a retrieval system, or transmitted, in any form or by any means without the prior written permission of the publisher, nor be otherwise circulated in any form of binding or cover other than that in which it is published and without a similar condition being imposed on the subsequent purchaser.

Hardback ISBN 978 0 7961 8300 2

www.tnco.co.za

CONTENTS

Introduction 1

Part 1 - Brand (YOU) Pty Ltd

Chapter 1 - Who's Who in the Networking Zoo– Introverts, Extroverts and Ambiverts 13
Chapter 2 - It all boils down to Neuroscience! The brains of Introverts, Extroverts anD Ambiverts are fundamentally different 25
Chapter 3 - Your Career Sweet spot 35
Chapter 4 - The CEO of Me PTY (Ltd) 57
Chapter 5 - What is the coffee stain on your brand? 71
Chapter 6 - Great brands need to stay relevant 85
Chapter 7 - You can't be brave if you're not well 103
Chapter 8 - Become a better Storyteller 111

Part 2 - Master the Art of Networking

Chapter 9 - The top characteristics of the best networkers 133
Chapter 10 - Who are the power brokers in networks? 153
Chapter 11 - What comes around goes around 177
Chapter 12 - The role of networks in your promotion 191
Chapter 13 - Where the rubber hits the road - Networking functions 215
Chapter 14 - Best small talk techniqueObserve, ask and reveal 229
Chapter 15 - Event etiquette– get the most out of events 237
Chapter 16 - Your elevator pitch 245
Chapter 17 - The art of the follow-up(an introvert superpower) 257
Chapter 18 - We're all in this together -Ubuntu 263

NETWORKING FOR **INTROVERTS**

"Hell is other people."

Jean-Paul Sartre

INTRODUCTION

Introverts are often seen as being too quiet and not "leadership material" in a business world where networking and building relationships is a key skill. It is a world that seems constructed for Extroverts.

I often meet people who are in a career cul-de-sac, despite their technical expertise. They say, "I'm really good at what I do, yet no-one other than my direct boss knows how good I am. I feel like I'm at a dead end and haven't been promoted recently. I hate going to functions and don't want to be seen as the schmoozer. I know I'm better than this, yet my career, position or salary isn't reflecting it."

If this sounds familiar, then YOU'RE IN THE RIGHT PLACE. I look forward to sharing some of the insights I've gained over the past 20 years, training and speaking to people all over the world about how to increase their business networks.

This is an A-Z manual on how to develop a powerful personal brand as an Introvert, and a kick-ass network that will serve you throughout your life. I've poured my heart and soul into this book, and shared every nugget I believe will be useful in both your personal life and your career.

I'm so looking forward to sharing this journey with you, as the skills of Personal Branding and Networking have the potential to be life changing.

NETWORKING FOR **INTROVERTS**

"If you want to go fast, go alone. If you want to go far, go together."

African proverb

INTRODUCTION

My Networking Journey

I originally studied to be an accountant. I was completely naïve and unaware how important a personal brand and network are in achieving real career fulfilment and success.

I believed hard work, being good at your job and putting in the hours, were the keys to developing your career. I hadn't yet realised that hard work, doing a good job and working long hours increasingly become a given in your career. Unfortunately, everyone else is doing that too!

Only later did I learn that these are not the factors that will distinguish you or earn you the promotions, salary increases and job satisfaction you deserve.

I felt invisible at university and I didn't enjoy my commerce degree. I had moved from a small town all-girls convent school to a large university with thousands of students. I felt intimidated by my fellow students – especially the male students – and became increasingly withdrawn and non-participative. I didn't feel comfortable putting up my hand and asking a question. I effectively became invisible.

There was nothing distinctive about me – I blended into the background. No lecturer or fellow student would be able to pick me out in a crowd.

Many Introverts have told me this is often how they feel when they're at work, big meetings, conferences or cocktail functions. They feel invisible, unheard and deeply uncomfortable when they're "put on the spot" to contribute.

NETWORKING FOR **INTROVERTS**

"It's not what you know, it's who you know.
It's not just who you know, but who knows about you."

Helen Nicholson

INTRODUCTION

I had one of my networking epiphanies at the age of 20. A university friend and I went back-packing in Southern Africa during our summer holidays. We stayed with family in Zimbabwe but in Malawi we were on our own. This was a real budget holiday – the entire six-week trip cost the equivalent of $100. We caught local transport and often ended up on buses amongst the chickens and goats. We stayed in very basic backpackers lodges.

There were no cellphones in 1990 and we had no credit cards. Malawi's financial infrastructure was under-developed and they relied on a travelling bank in rural areas. One day we got the timetable mixed up and landed up in Blantyre with no money. It remains one of my scariest life and travelling experiences. We were two young girls far from home in a foreign country where we didn't know anybody, didn't speak the language, had no cellphone access, no credit cards and NO MONEY!

The owner of the backpackers lodge saw how terrified we were and took pity on us. He allowed us to make one landline phone call to get help. We had to think very carefully about who to call. I knew my parents would be sympathetic but wouldn't know anyone who could help us. I ran through my network in my head. I finally settled on a school friend's father who had been to a well-known boys' private school and had a powerful alumni network. He imported goods into Africa and I knew he'd know someone who knew someone.

He did.
Thank heavens!
He saved the day.

An hour after my phone call $50 in cash was delivered to our lodge. The relief was immediate and profound.

NETWORKING FOR **INTROVERTS**

Me waiting for the bus, Malawi trip, December 1990

INTRODUCTION

The epiphany for me was that your connections can assist you in solving most of life's problems – both personally and professionally.

Everyone needs a network!
Lone rangers only get so far!

I grew up in a home where my parents didn't know people who knew people. When they had a problem they consulted the old-fashioned Yellow Pages - a printed business directory of companies (this was pre- Google!). For household repairs this often didn't work out well – they had to repeat repairs or were ripped off by unscrupulous service providers. Their network wasn't based on personal referrals or recommendations. They had grown up in homes where their parents didn't know people who knew people either – so this trait seemed to be handed down through generations.

I am the oldest of four children and we grew up in small town, Edenvale, near Johannesburg. It was a very middle-class home. There was a lot of love and independence but very few connections. My parents always struggled financially. Only in later years did I realise that their lack of networks and connections were linked to their financial hardship.

My mom was a teacher and my dad was a graphic artist. I went to an all-girls private school, only made possible because my mom taught at the same school.

My parents are introverted in nature, with small friendship groups. They still prefer staying at home to going out. I observed how they struggled personally and professionally as they carried their burdens alone. They They didn't have a tribe (network) to help them to make connections or provide access to resources.

"Networking is not about just connecting people. It's about connecting people with people, people with ideas, and people with opportunities."

Michele Jennae

INTRODUCTION

I've always had a hunch that Introverts are better at networking than Extroverts, as they are better listeners and more likely to follow-up after meeting a person.

Extroverts are often not great listeners. They tend to speak too much and may dominate conversations. They are also often not very good at following up after meeting a new person. They get energised by face- to-face interactions, but can then lose the person's contact details and forget to follow up.

I decided to put my hunch to the test and over the past four years have interviewed 253 people who identify as more Introverted than Extroverted, from all over the world.

This book confirms my hunch and presents the research:

"Introverts are better networkers than Extroverts (if they access their superpowers of listening, following up and building their personal brand and network intentionally)."

One of the other biggest realisations I've had after training thousands of people from all over the world for the past 20 years, is that networking is a learned skill. So, if you're more Introverted in nature, and didn't grow up in a home where your parents knew people who knew people, you still have the power to change your networking trajectory.

I did, and I now believe that my personal brand, connections and networks are now one of my biggest life and career assets.

You too have the power to develop your own treasure trove of connections and networks if you follow this process.

PART 1
BRAND (YOU)
PTY LTD

"You don't have to be an extrovert to be successful at networking. You just have to be an authentic introvert"

Susan Cain

CHAPTER 1
WHO'S WHO IN THE NETWORKING ZOO
– INTROVERTS, EXTROVERTS AND AMBIVERTS

The tired, outdated and narrow definitions of INTROVERT/EXTROVERT are that Introverts are quieter and feel more energised from spending time alone, while Extroverts are louder and derive their fulfillment and energy from being with others.

Extroverts are seen as more charismatic, charming and persuasive, while Introverts are seen as quieter, can be more creative and prefer to work alone.

These definitions are limiting from a networking perspective. We all exist on a spectrum between Introversion and Extroversion, which can largely be influenced by our circumstances.

If you've had a very social holiday, you may want to spend your first two nights back at home in your pyjamas watching Netflix. That doesn't make you an Introvert.

If you work in an open-plan office, even the biggest Extrovert may find the constant stimulation overwhelming and deliberately seek some down-time to brainstorm.

NETWORKING FOR **INTROVERTS**

THINGS **INTROVERTS** LOVE

- CANCELLED PLANS
- RAINY DAYS
- SOLO ACTIVITIES
- DEEP CONVERSATIONS
- DAYDREAMING
- TEXT MESSAGES
- RECHARGING
- HOME
- INTROSPECTION (THOUGHTS, IDEAS, FEELINGS, SNACKS, DOGS, MEANING OF LIFE)

@introvertmemes

WHO'S WHO IN THE **NETWORKING ZOO**

Being an Introvert also doesn't make you a hermit: Introverts can be social butterflies in their own quiet way, often with more one-on-one interactions or in small groups.

Two-thirds of people don't strongly identify as Introverts or Extroverts. These people are called Ambiverts, who have both Introverted and Extroverted tendencies.

So, for the purpose of this book, lets define who's who in the society zoo:

INTROVERTS

Energy Source
Introverts often recharge and gather energy from spending time alone or in low-stimulation environments. Large social gatherings or prolonged interactions can be draining for them.

Preference
They typically prefer time alone or one-on-one interactions and tend to be more reserved or reflective.

Misconceptions
Being an Introvert doesn't necessarily mean one is shy or socially anxious. It's more about where they draw their energy from. Some Introverts can be quite outgoing in the right circumstance, especially when they're talking about something they're passionate about.

Introverts gravitate towards the inner world of thought and feeling. They are experts at immersing themselves in their work and prefer to concentrate on one task at a time.

*"Being an introvert is not about where you get your energy. It's how you handle stimulation.
Introverts are energized by people too. We're just easily exhausted by loud parties, close talkers, and endless houseguests. I'm not antisocial.
I'm pro-quiet."*

Adam Grant

They need to process what is going on around them and replenish their energy levels by spending some much-needed time alone.

Author Jonathan Rauch, a self-confessed Introvert, sums it up perfectly. "Introverts are people who find other people tiring," he writes. "Extroverts are energised by people, and wilt and fade when they're alone. For Introverts, to be alone with our thoughts is as restorative as sleeping, as nourishing as eating."

In some ways Introverts are better equipped to connect with people. For one, they despise superficial small talk, preferring to have deeper, more meaningful one-on-one encounters. As a result, they may have fewer friendships than Extroverts but they are very close to people they count as friends.

It's difficult for an Extrovert to understand an Introvert. "Extroverts have little or no grasp of Introversion. They assume that company, especially their own, is always welcome. They cannot imagine why someone would need to be alone; they often take umbrage at the suggestion," says education expert Jill D Burruss.

Extroverts see Introversion as something that needs to be "fixed." Just ask anyone who has ever been coaxed "to come out of their shell," been given a pitying look while sitting alone in a public space, been asked whether they are depressed or been coerced into joining a group activity.

Instead of trying to be more Extroverted, my recommendation is to lean in and embrace the skills that come naturally to you – such as listening.

"Introverts are typically the friend or colleague you can call when you're upset or you have good news to share," says Beth Buelow, author of

NETWORKING FOR **INTROVERTS**

> **Friend:**
> Wanna hang out tomorrow?
>
> **Me:**
> I actually performed an activity yesterday. Please wait the three day recovery period to submit another inquiry.
>
> @introvertmemes

The Introvert Entrepreneur. Amplify your strengths and create success on your own terms.

The listening superpower is not to be underestimated in a world where it often seems that people are just waiting for their turn to talk. The reason why people turn to Introverts with good or bad news is that they're able to make the news about the person telling the story, and not turn it around and make it about themselves, as many Extroverts would do.

An Extrovert will typically jump in and start voicing their opinions before they've had time to really process what the other person has said. Introverts, on the other hand, don't dish out advice or weigh in until they've considered it fully. "We speak only when we have something to say, so there is a higher chance that we will make an impact with our words," explains Buelow.

Another superpower Introverts can harness as part of their personal brand is their observational skills. Their ability to notice shifts in body language and facial expressions makes them uniquely equipped to read the room, and better in general at conducting interpersonal relationships. "We notice things other people might not notice because they are too busy talking and processing out loud," says Buelow.

The difference between being Introverted and being Shy
Susan Cain, author of the excellent, best-selling book, *Quiet – The Power of Introverts in a World That Can't Stop Talking*, says people often assume that Introversion means being shy or anti-social.

It's really not that at all. It has to do with how different people respond to stimulation, including social stimulation. It's a nervous system issue, not merely a preference.

"Solitude matters, and for some people, it's the air they breathe."

Susan Cain

WHO'S WHO IN THE **NETWORKING ZOO**

Introverts feel at their most alive and at their most energised when they're in quieter, lower-key environments.

EXTROVERTS

Energy Source
Extroverts gain energy from being around others and are often drained by spending too much time alone.
Extroverts crave, need and depend on larger amounts of stimulation to feel at their best. This has huge implications for how we socialise.

Preference
They thrive in group settings, enjoy social events and often feel comfortable expressing themselves in larger gatherings.

Misconceptions
Being Extroverted doesn't mean one is always seeking attention or is superficial. They just tend to be more invigorated by social interactions.

AMBIVERTS

Energy Source
Ambiverts can draw energy from both social interactions and solitude. Their energy preferences can vary depending on the situation, mood or context.

Preference
They are flexible in social settings, being comfortable in both group interactions and alone time.

NETWORKING FOR **INTROVERTS**

Me, after too much peopling

@introvertmemes

WHO'S WHO IN THE **NETWORKING ZOO**

Misconceptions

Ambiversion isn't just being "in the middle" or "average" in terms of social interaction. Ambiverts have a broader spectrum of comfort, being able to tap into both Introverted and Extroverted tendencies depending on the situation.

Based on this understanding of the Introvert's superpowers, let's explore the world of the Introverts' Personal Brand, their networks and how they can amplify their natural strengths.

ACTIVITY

If you would like to find out if you are an Introvert, Extrovert or Ambivert, you can download the assessment with the QR code at the beginning of the book.

NETWORKING FOR **INTROVERTS**

CHAPTER 2
IT ALL BOILS DOWN TO NEUROSCIENCE!
THE BRAINS OF INTROVERTS, EXTROVERTS AND AMBIVERTS ARE FUNDAMENTALLY DIFFERENT

The reason why some people thrive on being the life and soul of the party, while others prefer to quietly curl up on the couch, alone with nothing more than a good book, scrolling on Instagram or watching Netflix is that the brains of Introverts and Extroverts are wired differently.

According to research published by *Medical Daily* in 2014, the best way to explain the differences between Introvert and Extrovert brains is by understanding how three chemicals in your brain work:
- Dopamine
- Adrenaline
- Acetylcholine

Dopamine is our "feel good" chemical. We love dopamine because it rewards us with feelings of happiness when we engage in activities we like. One of the reasons social media is so addictive is that we get a dopamine hit every time someone likes or shares our posts. The pleasurable effects of dopamine reinforce and motivate us to repeat these behaviours, which then stimulates the release of more dopamine.

Adrenaline, which is spiked by risk-taking, novelty and physical and environmental stimulation, causes more dopamine to be released.

Extrovert　　　　　　　　　Introvert

Extroverts have a low sensitivity to dopamine, so they require large amounts of it, while introverts are highly sensitive to dopamine. Too much of it makes them feel overstimulated.

IT ALL BOILS DOWN TO **NEUROSCIENCE!**

This is the first big difference between Introvert and Extrovert brains. Extroverts have more dopamine receptors in their brains. This means that Extroverts need more dopamine to feel happy, because they are less sensitive to it.

The more Extroverts talk, move and engage in stimulating activities, the more they feel dopamine's pleasant effects.

In contrast, Introverts have fewer dopamine receptors, so they are more sensitive to dopamine. This means that too much stimulation makes them feel overwhelmed and anxious.

Like dopamine, acetylcholine is also linked to pleasure but its effects are much more subtle. Acetylcholine makes us feel confident, relaxed and content. It also fuels our ability to think deeply, reflect and focus for long periods of time on one thing. When we engage in activities that are low-key, calming and mentally engaging we activate the release of acetylcholine.

For Extroverts, the pleasurable effect of acetylcholine pales in comparison to the jolt of happiness they experience from dopamine. However, Introverts crave acetylcholine. While Extroverts are out and about enjoying the benefits of all those dopamine receptors, Introverts are happily lounging at home watching their favourite series with a pleasant dose of acetylcholine.

In general, Ambiverts' levels of natural stimulation don't reach such great extremes, though they do fluctuate. Sometimes you may feel the need to seek out stimulation, while at other times you may avoid it. Knowing where you are on the Introvert/Ambivert/Extrovert spectrum and what your environment is like on any given day, helps you to know whether to seek out additional stimulation and chat to one more person or to go home early from a function.

"Don't let the noise of others' opinions drown out your own inner voice."

Steve Jobs

IT ALL BOILS DOWN TO **NEUROSCIENCE!**

Introverts and Extroverts prefer one side of their nervous system over the other side
The human nervous system has two sides:
- The Sympathetic side triggers the fight/flight response.
- The Para-Sympathetic side triggers the rest/digest mode.

The Sympathetic side of our nervous system is the equivalent of hitting the accelerator pedal of your car and the Para-Sympathetic side is like slamming on the brakes.

When your Sympathetic system is activated, your body gears up for action. Adrenaline is released, glucose energises muscles and oxygen increases. Areas of your brain that control thinking are turned off and dopamine increases alertness in the back of your brain, triggering the fight/flight response.

Extroverts, Ambiverts and Introverts all use both sides of the brain at different times. Introverts prefer using the Para-sympathetic side which slows and calms them down.

Conscious time spent in the Para-sympathetic part of your brain will increase your resilience in the stressful world we live in. This is a big part of Introverts' superpowers – to remain calm when everyone around them is losing their minds.

Pinball Brain in Action

**LONGER INTROVERT
DOPAMINE PATHWAY**

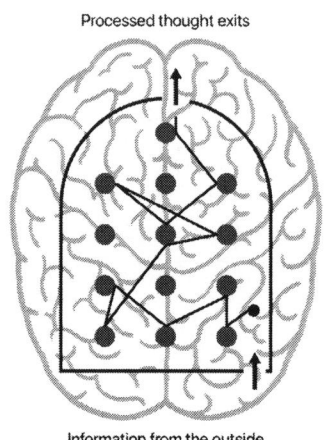

Processed thought exits

Information from the outside world enters the brain

**SHORTER EXTROVERT
DOPAMINE PATHWAY**

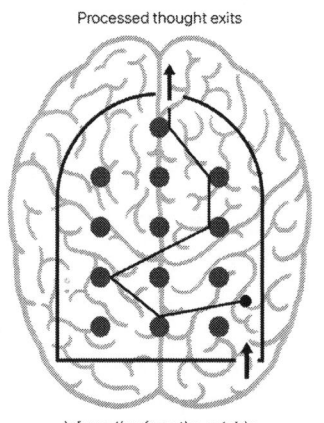

Processed thought exits

Information from the outside world enters the brain

IT ALL BOILS DOWN TO **NEUROSCIENCE!**

The Pinball Brain

Introverts and Extroverts also process stimuli in different ways.

When information from the outside world – someone's voice, a cellphone ringing, an alarm going off or email notifications popping into their Inbox – enters an Extrovert's brain, it travels a shorter pathway, passing through areas of the brain where taste, touch, sight and sound are processed.

This is what is known as the "Pinball" brain. Just as a ball pings around an old-fashioned pinball machine, so too do stimuli ping around an Extrovert's brain. This enables them to speak quickly and give the impression of being "quick thinkers", and they literally "think on their feet."

In reality, Extroverts could often do with more reflective time before speaking or making decisions which can appear rash, rushed, and not thought through.

For Introverts, stimulation travels through the same areas of the brain. The important difference is the time it takes before the information is thoroughly processed. This process takes much longer than the Extroverts' Pinball brain process.

This also explains why Introverts process information more slowly, thoroughly and deeply. This is why it sometimes takes Introverts longer to speak, react or make decisions.

NETWORKING FOR **INTROVERTS**

INTROVERT DREAM HOUSE

Library with reading nook

Glass ceiling tower for star gazing

Media room

Trap door

Art studio

Secret passageways for avoiding company

@introvertmemes

What Can Introverts Learn from This?

1. Self-Acceptance
Knowing that your Introverted tendencies have a biological neuroscience basis can help you accept and embrace your natural inclinations. There's nothing "wrong" with preferring quieter environments, deep one-on-one conversations and taking more time to respond and act.

2. Mindful Socialising
Being aware of your sensitivity to stimuli can help you plan social activities more sttrategically. For instance, you might prefer smaller gatherings, or you might find that having a quiet day before a big event helps you recharge and prepare.

3. Communication with Others
Understanding the brain chemistry behind Introversion can help Introverts communicate their needs to Extroverted friends, family members and colleagues. It provides a rationale for why they might prefer quieter environments or activities.

4. Self-Care
Recognising the need for downtime and quieter environments can encourage Introverts to prioritise self-care, ensuring they get the solitude they need to recharge.

NETWORKING FOR **INTROVERTS**

CHAPTER 3
YOUR CAREER **SWEET SPOT**

The process of discovering their Career Sweet Spot has caused previous exco-level delegates on our leadership training programmes to resign the next day, realising they are not working in their Career Sweet Spot Zone, and that time is running out for them to discover it.

It sounds very dramatic but understanding and building your career around what you're naturally good at and the work you were destined to do, is a revolutionary concept for many people.

I've observed big tipping points in people's careers when they discover their Career Sweet Spot. People begin to "get" you – your uniqueness, what makes you different and most importantly you begin to stand out in an increasingly cluttered market.

One of the biggest problems I see when speaking and training people is that they are often more in touch with their weaknesses than their strengths.

"What you are bad at actually doesn't interest people, and certainly shouldn't interest you. However accomplished you become in life, the things you are bad at will always outnumber the things you are good at. So don't let your limits knock your self-confidence. Put them to one side and push towards your strengths"

Richard Branson

Organisations reinforce this by having performance appraisals which are largely based on people's "development areas" or "weaknesses." Very seldom do leaders give you detailed feedback on your strengths, unless you ask for it.

As a double whammy career own-goal, we spend most of our career trying to fix our weaknesses, only to end up with very strong weaknesses. A great personal brand is never based on weaknesses.

If I had to ask you to list your top five strengths, my prediction is you'd have difficulty indentifying them with absolute clarity.

Whereas if I asked you to list your five weaknesses, you'd have no problems listing them, and you'd probably have more than five.

Can I say that again (in CAPITAL LETTERS – it's that important); *"YOUR CAREER SWEET SPOT IS BASED ON YOUR NATURAL STRENGTHS AND NOT YOUR WEAKNESSES."*

The ability to gain clarity around your Career Sweet Spot is a key attribute of being an Introvert. You can leverage a powerful personal brand, because you understand who you are, the value of leaning into your strengths and packaging your value.

Marcus Buckingham, the world-renowned strengths expert, researched hundreds of businesses and thousands of people worldwide and unequivocally demonstrated that top performers are those who focus on their strengths the majority of the time.

A strength is not what you are good at and a weakness is not what you are bad at. A strength is an activity that strengthens, motivates and engergises you. It draws you in. It makes time fly by while you're doing it, and it makes you feel strong, confident and successful.

"Without introverts, the world would be devoid of: the theory of gravity; the theory of relativity; W.B. Yeats's 'The Second Coming'; Chopin's nocturnes; Proust's In Search of Lost Time."

If you define a strength that way then the person best qualified to determine your strengths is you. You are the authority on which activities make you feel energised. Somebody else can judge your performance, or the quality and quantity of your work – but you and you alone can recognise your strengths.

This may seem obvious – focus on your strengths and you'll succeed. If we overlay clarity around your strengths with an understanding of what generation you are, things get more granular and interesting.

Generation Types:
- Baby Boomers are people born from 1946-1964
- Gen X: 1956-1980
- Millennials (Gen Y): 1981-1996
- Gen Z: 1994-2009
- Gen Alpha 1: 2010-2024
- Gen Beta will be born from 2025-2039

Take a moment to identify your generation type. This is the first step in identifing your strengths and then offering them out to the world.

According to Buckingham's research, Gen Y&Z show a marked tendency to overlook their strengths. Asked whether they will succeed professionally by fixing their weaknesses or by enhancing their strengths, an astounding 73% of Gen Y respondents (as compared to 55% overall) chose fixing their weaknesses as the key to success.

So what does this mean for Gen Ys and Gen Zs in the workforce? It means they need to double down on their strengths. Winning in the workplace means knowing who you are, where your greatest strengths lie and how to differentiate yourself.

"I've come to believe that each of us has a personal calling that's as unique as a fingerprint - and that the best way to succeed is to discover what you love and then find a way to offer it to others in the form of service, working hard, and also allowing the energy of the universe to lead you."

Oprah Winfrey

As the world changes dramatically – technology is evolving, AI (Artificial Intelligence) is making certain roles obsolete – your strengths are the one constant you can rely on. Specific skills may become redundant with change but your unique strengths are infinitely transferable and always relevant.

Management and talent consultants have recognised a Unique Strength Theory. If your productivity is seen as 100% of what you do, then on average 45% of it could be done better by someone else. Another 45% could be done by someone else at a similar level of competence. The remaining 10% is the work that only you can do. It's what makes you unique. Your top 10% is a combination of your personality, strengths and skills, and represents the work you were born to do.

Famous Introverts who tapped into their top 10% Career Sweet Spot to make a true impact include:
- Albert Einstein who was known for his depth and clarity of thought. He had the ability to look at a problem from all angles and develop innovative (and often unexpected) solutions.
- Steve Wozniak, co-founder of Apple and a well-known Introvert, who worked outside the limelight, engineering technology breakthroughs for Apple. Wozniak and Steve Jobs, (the other Apple co-founder and Extrovert) were the perfect leadership combination.

I'm currently attending an excellent coaching programme, for entrepreneurs, *Strategic Coach*, in London. One of the exercises we were encouraged to do was a two week time-log of our activities, rating our feelings of flow and energy while doing each activity.

"Finding your passion isn't just about careers and money. It's about finding your authentic self, the one you've buried beneath other people's needs."

Kristin Hannah

They were trying to get us as entrepreneurs to distinguish between our Career Sweet Spot and activities we felt we were good at. The difference between what you're good at and what you're excellent at is subtle, nuanced and VERY IMPORTANT!

My epiphany when asked questions like:
- When do you feel most in flow?
- What are you doing when you feel that you make the most impact?
- When are your energy levels the highest?

was that my Career Sweet Spot is speaking to large audiences, seeing the lights going on in their eyes and feeling that I make a difference in the message that I share. It's not facilitating smaller groups and it's not getting involved in the nitty gritty of running a business.

My top strength is *Futurism* according to the Gallup Strengths Finder (see link in the bibliography) which I strongly suggest you do. According to Gallup, I'm excellent at seeing opportunities for the business and charting a course forward. I have no Top 10 execution strengths, so I need a very good team around me to execute on my ideas. This is a classic entrepreneur strengths profile.

Distinguishing between what you're good at and what your Career Sweet Spot is, is part of our life's purpose. In my experience, I'd be surprised if people have discovered it by the age of 30. I believe people can be in the experimentation phase, trying different careers and roles, until they're around 35.

I meet many talented people who are miserable in their jobs and my feedback to them is, "It's a gift." Having clarity about what you don't like fast-tracks your journey to your Career Sweet Spot.

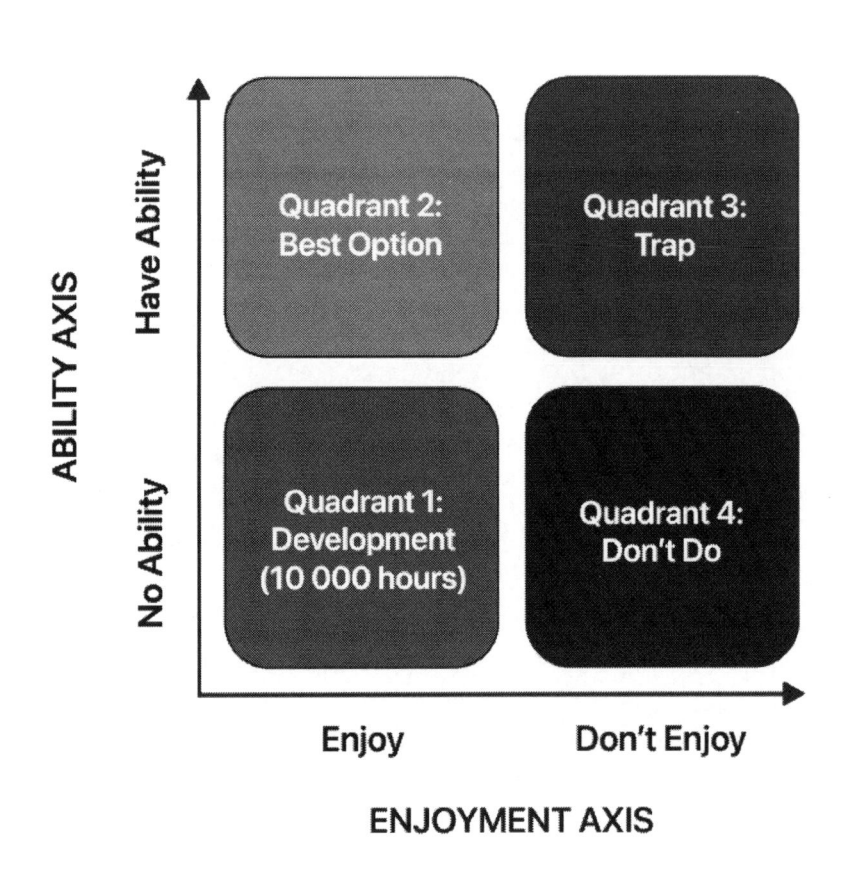

NETWORKING FOR **INTROVERTS**

ABILITY AXIS

Have Ability | Quadrant 2: Best Option | Quadrant 3: Trap
No Ability | Quadrant 1: Development (10 000 hours) | Quadrant 4: Don't Do

Enjoy | Don't Enjoy

ENJOYMENT AXIS

YOUR CAREER **SWEET SPOT**

If you're reading this and your Career Sweet Spot is feeling very foreign, or unknown, do not despair or resign immediately. Come on this journey with me – we spend 70% of our waking hours at work and we deserve to fulfil our purpose through our work.

As an Introvert you have incredible strengths that are increasingly needed in this turbulent world:
- Excellent listening skills
- Thinking before speaking
- Uncanny observational skills - Introverts notice subtle body language cues and what's not being said
- Compassionate leadership skills
- Deep friendships
- Creative thinking
- Thoughtful networking through deep connections
- The ability to empower teams and let others shine

The key point is to get absolute clarity around your Introvert strengths and package them as part of your personal brand. Then communicate your brand to your target market (through your network) in a way that feels authentic and comfortable to you.

To further expand on the 10% Career Sweet Spot Zone, I've included a model to enable you to plot where you believe you're currently at.

In this Career Sweet Spot model you will see a horizontal Enjoyment axis and a vertical Ability axis. We spend time in each of the quadrants during our days but the more time we spend in Quadrant 2, the more likely we are to be happy, fulfilled and have a powerful personal brand.

"Introverts are uniquely gifted and skilled- as leaders, artists, scientists and entrepreneurs- as long as they have the opportunity to get fired up about something they believe in."

Susan Cain

In **Quadrant 1** we have low ability, but high enjoyment; this is where we need to practise something to get better and improve our ability. I love to cook but wasn't very good at it until I went for lessons and followed recipes. I can now produce a delicious meal because of hours spent at a stove – I wasn't a natural in the first place though. Practice does make perfect – although I'm no MasterChef, I'm competent and I enjoy it. So I've moved from **Quadrant 1** to **Quadrant 2** with my cooking.

In Malcolm Gladwell's book "Outliers", he estimates that it takes around 10 000 hours to become a master or subject matter expert. He used the examples of the Beatles pop band and Bill Gates, the founder of Microsoft, who practised their respective crafts for 10 000 hours in their late teens and early twenties. As a result, they were able to move into their Career Sweet Spots of music and technology relatively early in their lives. They were ahead of everyone else as they had been focusing on their Career Sweet Spot earlier and for a longer time.

In **Quadrant 2**, people hit their Career Sweet Spot when they enjoy something and they are good at it.

For Introverts, finding their Career Sweet Spot can be a life-transforming experience enabling them to leverage their strengths and minimise the challenges associated with being an Introvert in a predominantly Extroverted world.

> People always tell introverts to be more talkative and leave their comfort zones, yet no one tells extroverts to shut up and make the zone comfortable
>
> No, no. He's got a point.
>
> @introvertmemes

Here's what Introverts can learn from identifying and operating within their Career Sweet Spot:

1. **Value of Deep Work:**
   Introverts often excel at tasks that require deep concentration, reflection and independent work. Careers that allow for periods of uninterrupted focus can be particularly rewarding for introverts. Such careers might include roles like writing, programming, research or design.

2. **Strength in one-on-one interaction:**
   While Introverts might find large group dynamics draining, they thrive in one-on-one settings. This can be an asset in careers like consulting, coaching or mentoring where deep, meaningful connections are more valuable than broad, superficial interactions.

3. **Passion drives excellence:**
   When Introverts find careers that align with their intrinsic passions, they become highly dedicated and efficient workers. Their passion- driven focus can make them experts in their field.

4. **The Power of Preparation:**
   Introverts often feel more comfortable when they're well prepared. By recognising this trait, Introverts can select and excel in careers where meticulous planning and preparation are valued.

5. **Quality over quantity:**
   Introverts can shine in roles that value depth and quality of work over sheer volume or visibility. Their natural tendency to reflect before acting can result in high-quality outputs.

> **"Don't think of introversion as something that needs to be cured."**

Susan Cain

6. Remote and flexible work:
With the rise of remote/hybrid work opportunities, Introverts can find roles that allow them to work in their preferred environments. This can lead to increased productivity and job satisfaction.

7. Continuous Learning:
Many Introverts are life-long learners, driven by a natural curiosity. Roles that allow for continuous skill acquisition, knowledge enhancement and growth can be especially fulfilling.

8. Self-promotion in a non-boastful authentic way:
While self-promotion might not come naturally to many Introverts, understanding their Career Sweet Spot can empower them to advocate for themselves. They can learn to highlight their strengths and achievements in ways that resonate with their personality, instead of emulating Extroverted more "in-your-face" promotion styles.

By understanding and aligning with their Career Sweet Spot, Introverts can carve out a professional path that not only brings financial rewards but also provides deep personal and emotional satisfaction.

Quadrant 3 (page 43) is the zone that traumatises many people in our workshops: the Trap Zone. People find themselves trapped in this zone, where they have ability but no enjoyment, because they lack clarity about their Career Sweet Spot.

Unfortunately, when people don't have clarity about their Career Sweet Spot, other people often impose their clarity about your career on you.

If you showed a particular flare for a particular skill early in your career, you can be boxed into that role. Unless you have absolute clarity as to

"The two most important days in your life are the day you are born and the day you find out why."

Mark Twain

what else you enjoy and are good at, your career will go off on a certain trajectory, based on your boss's clarity. That's often why I meet people in their forties and fifties feeling unfulfilled in their work – they lack clarity about their Career Sweet Spot.

Quadrant 4 is not a place many people spend a lot of time in. This is where they don't enjoy the activity and have very little ability, so we're not going to spend time focusing on that quadrant from a personal branding growth perspective.

From a career development perspective the two most important quadrants are **Quadrants 2 and 3.**

They have the most important influence on your ability to truly connect to your talents and then align those talents to your career. That clarity results in your moving from **Quadrant 3** (Trap Zone) to **Quadrant 2** (Sweet Spot). That is where you will make the most impact.

I'm not saying ignore your weaknesses, especially as you grow and develop in your career. We need to pay attention to things we are not good at. The most important issue from a Career Sweet Spot perspective is the percentage of time people spend in these zones.

If you're spending 60-80% of your time working in your weakness zone **(Quadrant 3 & 4),** I guarantee that you're going to feel un-energised and flat most of the time. Our energy is sending us messages all the time. Does the activity drain or energise you? An ideal playing-to-your- strengths day should be 60-80% of your time spent in your Career Sweet Spot Zone and 20-40% of time focusing on your weaknesses. We all go through tough times in our jobs. If your colleague is on leave or if you're short-staffed then you may have to spend more time focusing on your weaknesses.

NETWORKING FOR **INTROVERTS**

HOW INTROVERTS MAKE FRIENDS

- They don't
- An extrovert found them, liked them, and adopted them

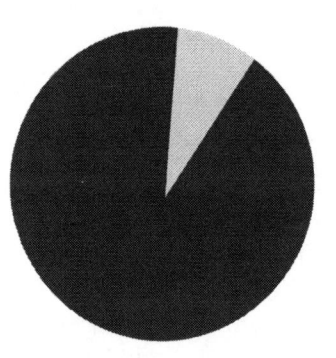

@introvertmemes

If this carries on too long, it will eventually lead to you battling to get out of bed in the morning. In my experience, if that goes on for longer than six months then it's a perfect indicator it's time for a career change.

INTROVERT ACTIVITIES TO GET CLARITY ABOUT YOUR STRENGTHS:
- Conduct an energy audit for two weeks – log each activity you complete and rate your energy level with 10 being the highest and 1 the lowest for each activity. You'll get a very clear picture of how much time and energy you're spending in your Career Sweet Spot Zone.
- Complete a strengths assessment such as Gallup Strengths Finder https://www.gallup.com/cliftonstrengths
- Control your working environment based on your strength insights. If you're in an open-plan office, find ways to define your personal space to increase your ability to stay focussed on what you're excellent at. Go and work in a smaller room on a regular basis when you need to do deep work and avoid distractions.
- Communicate your value. Keep a record of your accomplishments and make sure you communicate how you work best and how you can add the most value to your line manager.
- Leverage and get really clear about which of the Introvert strengths discussed on Page 48 & 50 you identify more with.

ACTIVITY

Download an Energy Audit tracker through the QR code at the beginning of the book.

CHAPTER 4
THE CEO OF **ME PTY (LTD)**

You need to find a way to make a meaningful contribution, add value and stand out. That's the only way to survive and thrive!

Powerful Introverts work intentionally on their personal brands. Well- developed personal brands don't happen by accident. These Introverts have an innate understanding that a strong personal brand has the power to transform their careers.

You already have a brand as you're reading this book today.

As Jeff Bezos, the founder of Amazon, once said, "Your brand is what people say about you when you're not in the room." However, most people have not thought of themselves as brands – they get on with their work, hoping that someone will notice them. They may be talented, but they are not well known.

"Be Yourself, everyone else is taken."

Oscar Wilde

THE CEO OF **ME PTY (LTD)**

As my friend, colleague and *Harvard Business Review* contributor Niven Postma says:

"Invisible contributions have no value from a political perspective."

True story.

I can't tell you how many Introverts I meet who tell me, "My work should speak for itself." They wonder why their careers are stuck and they're not getting the recognition or promotions they feel they deserve. My response is to urgently launch the equivalent of a PR campaign for your brand in a way that feels authentic to you and challenges you at the same time.

The biggest personal branding risk to an Introvert is being a no-name brand.

No-name grocery brand purchases are generally grudge purchases. We buy them mainly for financial reasons. They have little or no emotional attachment for us.

If you apply the same grocery no-name brand theory to people, the same lessons apply.

I learned this very powerfully when I worked at a leading business school. I started a job that no-one had filled for over a year, so I had to catch up on a huge backlog of work. The academics at the school gathered for tea every day at 10.30am to touch base and discuss their projects. I decided I was far too busy to join them. As a result of not being at the daily staff tea, I became a no-name brand. I had become invisible. I had a direct report to the Director, so he knew what projects I was busy with, but my colleagues didn't.

NETWORKING FOR **INTROVERTS**

"In the past, knowledge workers with average skills doing an average job, could earn an average lifestyle. But today, average is officially over. Being average just won't earn you what it used to. It can't when so many employers have so much access to remote workers, Artificial Intelligence, cheap software and cheap automation. Being average won't get you noticed. It doesn't matter what field you're in"

Fast Company 2024

After a guest lecture to a group of MBA students, a young Introvert engineer, Lukas, approached me. He was one of only six engineers in the country with his specialisation and he didn't feel the need to build his personal brand or his network. He was technically excellent at what he did and had a prestigious job at the national power utility company. The CEO knew him personally and had recognised his expertise.

My response was that in my experience technical expertise would only take him so far. I said it would be interesting to see where his career strategy would take him.

I bumped into him about four years later at a conference. He asked me if I recognised him. I replied that I did, as our conversation had really stayed with me. He had been so certain that personal branding and networking were not for him, and a complete waste of time.

It was sad to see the changes in him. He'd aged significantly – he looked older and sadder. He had lost his arrogance and the certainty he'd had about his career. He told me that shortly after we'd met, the CEO he'd known and had a long-standing working relationship with had left the organisation. The new CEO brought in his own people, with whom he had worked before. The new CEO didn't know Lukas or have any details about his skillset or expertise!

Lukas watched his colleagues get promoted over him and earn more money. They had invested in building strategic networking relationships both with the new CEO and with their other stakeholders. As a result, they had a clear personal brand. Lukas had become invisible – effectively a no-name brand.

"The secret to life is to put yourself in the right lighting. For some, it's a Broadway spotlight; for others, a lamplit desk."

Susan Cain

It was a powerful lesson about neglecting your personal brand and your relationships. Many Introverts have said to me over the course of my career, "I shouldn't have to schmooze or brown-nose for my boss, colleagues or company to appreciate me."

I tell them the story of Lukas.

I'm not advocating schmoozing. What I am advocating is that you intentionally package yourself so people know your value. Take control of your personal brand, or someone else will.

The other problem with relying on your work to speak for itself is that your brand rests in the hands of one person – your line manager. If you have a line manager that doesn't have well-developed EQ or doesn't have a vested interest in your development then it's essential you communicate your key achievements to your stakeholders, regularly and consistently.

Even if your line manager is completely invested in your development, you still need to communicate your value more broadly. It's dangerous to have all your personal branding eggs in one basket.

Italia Boninelli, a well-regarded HR director with vast experience across various industries, gave our delegates this very important piece of advice. Keep a notebook/folder on your phone labelled "Key achievements" with you at all times. Whenever someone gives you positive feedback on a project/task or you accomplish something, make a note of it. If we don't do this we generally only consider our achievements at our annual performance appraisals.

"Your brand is the gateway to your true work. You know you are here to do something, to create something, or to help others in some way. The question is, how can you set up your life and work so that you can do it?"

Dave Buck

From a personal branding perspective, communicating your key achievements is a vital part of your personal branding toolkit. You don't have to communicate what you're busy with or your wins in an arrogant or boastful way. My suggestion is to say to stakeholders, "I just want to keep you updated". This strategy makes many Introverts feel a lot more comfortable with communicating their value and their contributions.

Your personal brand is the sum of every touch point you have with all your stakeholders:
- Every email you reply to (or don't)
- How punctual you are to meetings
- How you dress
- Your body language
- Whether you spell-check everything before you hit send
- How you speak and present
- Whether you get back to people (or don't)

All of the above contribute to either enhancing or breaking down your brand.

We like product and food brands that are consistent – consistency builds trust. I have a favourite peanut butter brand. I have an expectation it's going to taste the same as the last time I bought it. That's what keeps me loyal to that brand.

In exactly the same way, the more consistent and authentic we are, the more powerfully received our personal brand will be.

When your name is mentioned amongst your family, friends and colleagues there are words that come to people's mind to describe you. Your personal brand already exists. The big question is, "Do you know what your personal brand is amongst your different stakeholders?"

"Personal branding is about managing your name — even if you don't own a business — in a world of misinformation, disinformation, and semi-permanent Google records."

Tim Ferriss

THE CEO OF ME PTY (LTD)

When I first got involved in this work my twin daughters were eight years old. I checked in with them about how they perceived me, their mother, from a branding point of view. I asked them, "If you had to describe mommy in one word, what would it be?"

Identically they looked up at me and said "rushed." They elaborated, saying "You always pat your wrist (indicating an imaginary watch) and you always say to us, 'Hurry up, we're going to be late'." I was both devastated and amused that this was my mother brand, as perceived by my children. I didn't want my tombstone to say, "Here lies Helen – she was rushed" – it was definitely not the legacy I wanted. I then actively worked to change their perception – I changed the watches, clocks and my phone to always run 10 minutes ahead of time.

I now check in with my clients, my husband, my family and my children once a year about their current perceptions of my personal brand. Last year my daughters told me that I was "kind and bossy" – I'm not sure how much progress we've made but at least it wasn't "rushed" again.

When you finish this chapter I'd like to encourage you to send out a WhatsApp message to six key stakeholders saying:

"I'm going through a personal branding exercise and I'd value your feedback:

"If you had to describe me in one word what would it be?"

For this exercise choose a family member, colleague, friend, boss, internal/external client and people whose opinion you value.

"Your personal brand is the single most important investment you can make in your life."

Steve Forbes

SEEK OUT PATTERNS IN PAST PERFORMANCE

Dorie Clark, in her excellent book, *Re-inventing YOU*, encourages people to gather hard data about how others perceive them, along with the anecdotal WhatsApp messages.

If you've applied to graduate or leadership programmes, you may have access to recommendation or nomination letters/emails others have written for you, which are a treasure trove of intelligence.

Gather the material and step back. You're looking for patterns – if everyone comments on your bad spelling, your inability to delegate and your disorganisation, then you should take it seriously!

You're not looking for once-off comments – you're looking for patterns and trends.
- What adjectives, both positive and negative, do people use to describe you?
- What skills do they say you have or lack?
- What aspects about you or your brand are the most frequently talked about?
- Are there any aspects of you that are seen as unique or unusual?

Most importantly – do you like what you hear?

What words do you want people to link you with?

ACTIVITY

Download a Key Achievements tracker with the QR code at the beginning of the book.

NETWORKING FOR **INTROVERTS**

CHAPTER 5
WHAT IS THE **COFFEE STAIN** ON YOUR BRAND?

Vanessa Bluen, my great friend, mentor and business soul-mate, tells a wonderful story of being on an aeroplane on a business trip. As they were taxiing down the runway, her tray-table flopped down and she saw a coffee stain on it. What went through her mind as a client of that airline was, "If there's a coffee stain on the tray-table, then they clearly haven't checked the cleanliness of the plane. If they haven't checked the cleanliness of the plane, then they possibly haven't checked the engine either."

Immediately she went from feeling safe to feeling unsafe.

That same process happens if you are at a restaurant and the path to the bathroom takes you through the kitchen. If you see it is unclean, you immediately worry about the quality and hygiene of the food being served.

"In the business world, your reputation is currency. Even small stains can leave a lasting mark."

Harvey Mackay

WHAT IS THE **COFFEE STAIN** ON **YOUR BRAND?**

Just as there may be physical coffee stains on tray tables, there are also metaphoric coffee stains on us as people. A coffee stain from a personal branding perspective is a negative behaviour which can prevent your brand from developing to the next level. You may be conscious of it or not.

I learned a few years ago that my coffee stain is "slow response to email" after getting feedback from various people. I was a one-finger typist, so I was slow to respond and I receive a lot of mail. I just never seemed to catch up. People gave me feedback that as a personal branding and networking strategist, I was not walking my talk. I actively worked on my coffee stain and got my average response time down to 24 hours.

Examples of coffee stains I've observed are :

1. Punctuality (or lack thereof):
You become famous for being late. On virtual calls being two or three minutes late is very noticeable.

2. Your LinkedIn Profile:
LinkedIn has become even more important now with the increase of remote work. Before anyone meets you, they're going to Google you and the first thing that appears in a Google search is your LinkedIn profile. It's not just a job placement site – it's become the shopfront of your personal brand.

- Do you have a clear, up-to-date head and shoulders pic?
- LinkedIn is not a CV dumping site – it's an opportunity to package and communicate your personal brand value.
- You need recommendations from colleagues, bosses or clients. The best way to get more recommendations is to give them generously to people you've worked with and rate their performance.
- Is your profile robust and fully complete?

"Your personal brand is like a credit score. A single misstep can tarnish it, but consistent good actions can enhance it."

Dorie Clark

- The LinkedIn algorithm works based on prioritising people with 500 connections or more. So if you're looking for a merchant banker that specialises in mergers and acquisitions in London, the algorithm will rank the connections based on how many connections they have. People with 500-plus connections will automatically go to the top of your LinkedIn search, versus their competitor with 450 connections. You need to get to more than 500 connections as quickly as possible, so you don't run the risk of being invisible.
- Join at least one international industry group so you keep up to date with trends/issues in your industry.

I allocate two 15-minute weekly slots to growing my LinkedIn profile. I sit down with a cup of coffee, post/share two articles every week, check out the comments in groups I'm part of and I send personal messages to people I want to connect with.

LinkedIn is a very important personal branding tool. It's not for your friends and family, it's there to develop your peer-to-peer professional network.

3. Visibility online:
I spoke to the senior partners at a large auditing company last year. It was at the end of the day. No-one had their cameras on during my session. The COO (Chief Operating Officer) switched on her camera at the end of my presentation to say thank you and facilitate a Q&A session. She was sitting on her unmade bed at five o'clock in the afternoon.

"*A strong consistent brand, built up over time is one of the best guarantees of future earnings.*"

Marketing Review 2020

I will probably never get to meet this person as she's based in another country but her personal brand was compromised for me, and the other 450 colleagues on the call too.

As a presenter I like to see the reaction of my audience, as it energises me and enables me to make a stronger presentation. As for the unmade bed, it is hard to avoid the opinion that there may be a correlation between sloppy personal habits and sloppiness at work.

Work on your showing-up skills, always have your camera on during virtual meetings and be camera-ready. It shows respect for your personal brand as well as for your colleagues.

4. The words that come out of your mouth can be a potential coffee stain:
Do you complain a lot or speak negatively about other people, your company or your country? You will be judged by how you leave people feeling after you've had a conversation with them.

Energy is contagious – make sure that the energy/words that come out of your mouth are not potential coffee stains.

5. How you dress can also be a potential coffee stain:
Are you overly casual, wearing tracksuits every day?
Do you wear revealing clothes?

The sad reality is that 70% of people's perception of you is visual, so your clothing needs to match the brand you want to be known for. I believe you should always dress for the next level of your career.

"In building a personal brand, it's not about avoiding mistakes entirely but about handling them with grace and integrity."

Unknown

INTROVERT-SPECIFIC COFFEE STAINS:

1. Talking too much or talking too little

Extroverts tend to appear as quick thinkers and express their opinions vocally because of the pinball brain I referenced in Chapter Two, whereas Introverts often think of what they wanted to say after the meeting is over.

My recommendation is to go into a meeting with a question or a contribution prepared. Do your research and consult stakeholders before the meeting. You are then prepared and will make a well-thought-out, considered contribution which is always valued. If you're at a meeting you should have something to contribute, otherwise you shouldn't be there.

2. Your voice and whether people listen to you or not

I've had many delegates complain that they've pitched an idea at meetings that hasn't been acknowledged – but then later in the same meeting someone else pitches the same idea, but verbalises it differently, and it is heard and acknowledged. This can be enormously frustrating.

If this is something that happens to you my advice is to lean forward when you speak, fully engage your body and say, "I have two/three important points to make." Say them succinctly, bullet point them and then end with a call to action, "My recommendation is …."

3. Reluctance to Network

Many Introverts find networking events or social mixers intimidating, stressful and draining. If you don't push yourself to participate, you might miss out on valuable opportunities or connections. The more you practice the easier it will become.

"Your personal brand is a reflection of who you are. Every stain on it tells a story — make sure it's one of resilience and learning."

Anonymous

4. Perceived lack of enthusiasm

Because Introverts don't always show their excitement or passion, others may misinterpret your demeanour as a lack of interest or motivation.

My suggestion is to deliberately smile more both at meetings and social gatherings.

5. Avoidance of self-promotion

Many Introverts are uncomfortable talking about their achievements, which can hinder recognition and advancement in their careers.

Adopt the newsy approach we spoke about earlier – at least once a month say to your stakeholders, "I just want to keep you updated" and share your wins and contributions.

6. Over-reliance on written communication

While Introverts might excel at written communication, over-relying on it can sometimes make you seem distant or impersonal.

Don't send long emails when a phone-call or a visit to someone's desk will be more effective. The email is then only sent as a record of the discussion.

7. Struggle with impromptu interactions

Introverts often prefer planned, structured interactions and may feel caught off-guard by unexpected conversations or demands. This might make them seem unprepared or hesitant.

NETWORKING FOR **INTROVERTS**

WHAT IS THE **COFFEE STAIN** ON **YOUR BRAND?**

My advice is to carve out weekly "walk the floor" time, when you deliberately spend an hour walking around your building connecting and chatting to people in the business. Again, the more you practice the easier it will get.

I share my favourite small-talk technique with you in Chapter Fourteen, which will be very helpful here.

ACTIVITY

Download a Coffee Stain tracker with the QR code at the beginning of the book.

NETWORKING FOR **INTROVERTS**

CHAPTER 6
GREAT BRANDS NEED TO STAY RELEVANT

I first heard about the concept of Relevancy Quotient (RQ) at a conference I attended at Google a few years ago. The speaker, a leader at Google, said that prospective employees were assessed on various criteria, one of the most important being RQ (Relevancy Quotient). Through your RQ score, a potential employer is specifically looking for a growth mindset, your potential to be change-agile and your ability to remain relevant.

We're all familiar with EQ (Emotional Quotient) but I believe RQ is increasingly what is gettingandkeeping people in jobs in the competitive jobs market of today. The ideal employee would have the combination of a good RQ and EQ. Your ability to stay relevant will future-proof your career, whether you're an Introvert, Ambivert or Extrovert. RQ cuts across personality styles and industries. Change is a given, so we all need to be able to grow, adapt, and keep up with the pace of change.

"The world is changing very fast. Big will not beat small anymore. It will be the fast beating the slow."

Rupert Murdoch

GREAT BRANDS NEED TO **STAY RELEVANT**

You only need to look at brands like Nokia, Blackberry or Kodak to see the price companies pay for not staying relevant.

I know it may sound like a contradiction – I've emphasised consistency in my previous chapter, and now I'm emphasising your ability to change and adapt. You need to be consistent in consistently upping your game from a skills, hobby and mindset perspective to ensure you're always an impactful, growing and influential brand.

Professionals with high RQ are more likely to identify and seize opportunities for career advancement. This may include promotions, new job opportunities or the chance to work on innovative projects.

Keeping skills and knowledge up to date can significantly boost a person's confidence in their professional capabilities. It also leads to greater job satisfaction as people feel more competent and able to contribute meaningfully to their company or field.

When people are up-to-date with the latest trends and technologies they are often better positioned to think creatively and bring new ideas to their work.

I observed the lack of RQ in action with my dad's career. He studied to be a commercial artist and designed line drawing ads for his clients. When desktop publishing and graphic design came in, he didn't learn the new tech. His job eventually became redundant and, more importantly, he lost his confidence. I observed how that led to a life-long financial struggle caused by an inability to stay relevant.

"*Relevance is not something you can buy. It's earned by staying authentic, updated, and consistently delivering value.*"

Bernard Kelvin Clive

INTROVERTS AND RQ

Introverts, just like anyone else in business, need to stay relevant in their careers for the reasons we've discussed:
- Job security
- Career advancement
- Personal growth

However there are specific nuances that speak to why staying relevant might hold particular significance for Introverts:

1. Introverts need to amplify their presence in a noisy world

In a work environment often dominated by Extroverts, staying relevant through knowledge and expertise allows Introverts to amplify their presence and their contributions without necessarily stepping too far out of their comfort zones.

Their expertise enables them to be heard and recognised for their skills and insights, rather than their ability to out-talk others.

2. Introverts tend to excel in thoughtful, well-considered communication

When they do choose to speak up, their contributions are impactful and valuable, making the most of their natural pre-disposition towards depth over breadth in conversations and work.

3. Introverts can network on their own terms when they stay relevant

By being well-informed and skilled, Introverts can more easily find common ground with others in their field, facilitating networking opportunities that are more meaningful and less energy draining than traditional networking might be.

> *"In a constantly changing world, the most dangerous thing you can do is stay the same."*

Reid Hoffman

4. Building confidence
Continuously updating their knowledge and skills can significantly boost Introverts' confidence in professional settings. This confidence can empower them to take on new challenges and put themselves forward for opportunities they might otherwise have shied away from.

5. Adapting to remote and digital work environments
The shift towards remote work and digital communication platforms can work very well to the Introverts' advantage, offering them a way to engage and collaborate on their own terms. Staying tech-savvy and relevant ensures they can maximise these benefits, enhancing their productivity and work satisfaction.

When I returned from the Google conference, I started to set yearly RQ goals for myself both professionally and personally. My criteria was that the RQ goal had to scare me and challenge me out of my comfort zones.

In 2021 I set a personal RQ goal of learning how to touch-type (remember my coffee stain was not replying to people's emails and not being able to touch type was a significant contributor to that). At our school you had to choose between maths and typing as a subject, and I'd chosen maths. I had been a one-finger typist for years until 2021. During Covid I decided I was going to conquer this skills gap, as we all spent more time at home. I used the Apple typing tutorial and practiced every day for three months.

I realised I have very poor co-ordination, especially in my hands. I really didn't like learning how to touch type and my fingers took strain, but I persevered. Now I can type 50 words per minute and it's been a writing game-changer. I should've done it years ago!

"Introverts, in contrast, may have strong social skills and enjoy parties and business meetings, but after a while wish they were home in their pyjamas. They prefer to devote their social energies to close friends, colleagues, and family. They listen more than they talk, think before they speak, and often feel as if they express themselves better in writing than conversation."

Susan Cain

My professional RQ goal that same year was to start a podcast. My team and I knew nothing about podcasting – but it's amazing what you can learn. We launched the She Ignites podcast where I interviewed successful women and showcased their stories. We're going to launch the second series later in 2024 – so watch this space!

In 2022 my personal RQ goal was to learn how to dance with my husband. We are both very bad dancers, and I can't tell you we've improved greatly but we have a lot of fun and we laugh a lot. Our dance instructor needs a medal for his patience, but we persevere!

The most important point about RQ is to start something where you're a beginner. Often, especially as we get older, we stick to what we know and don't do new things. This means that our brains don't make new connections.

Neuroplasticity is a fundamental concept in neuroscience that refers to the brain's ability to change and adapt as a result of experiences. Engaging in new activities stimulates neuroplasticity, encouraging the brain cells to make new connections.

Whenever I start something new I notice how hard it is and how deeply uncomfortable I feel. That's OK! I've realised it gets better and you improve with perseverance. The currency of relevance is bravery. If your RQ goal doesn't scare you, then it's not the right RQ activity.

In 2022 my professional RQ goal was to write my third book, *Mindfulness: How to stay sane in an insane world,* and self-publish it. My team and I learned so much about editing, typesetting, printing and how to publish on Amazon, Kindle and Audible. It was tough but so worth it, because as we speak the book is in its fourth print run and has been a best-seller. The hard work paid off – it always does!

"Your brand is a combination of a thousand tiny gestures. Make sure they are consistently updated and relevant to your audience."

Alexander Isley

GREAT BRANDS NEED TO **STAY RELEVANT**

In 2023 my personal RQ goal was to have a freezing cold shower every morning after my bath. Plunging into the ice-cold water every morning is known as the Wim-Hof method. Wim Hof is a Dutch man who has done fascinating research on how cold water decreases the inflammation in your body. Inflammation, he believes, is the root cause of cancer and many other diseases.

Over the course of 2023 I watched my precious friend, Antenocia Gitzner, die of pancreatic cancer. She took her last breath at exactly midnight on 31 December 2023 as the fireworks started. It was a fitting end to the life of an incredible woman, one of my favourite people in the world.

I started these cold-water showers as a tribute to my friend, and because I don't want to get cancer either. Having these freezing cold showers was really tough, especially in winter. What I did realise when you're doing hard things is how important your "why" is.

Tapping into the love I had for my friend enabled me to endure temporary discomfort in that shower.

I would strongly encourage you to tap into your why of relevancy when doing hard things.
   - Why is this important to you?
   - What will happen if you don't push yourself to do it?
   - What will happen if you stop?

The emotional connection with your why, helps you to stick to the new RQ habit, despite the initial discomfort.

"How do you eat an elephant? Piece by piece."

Anonymous

GREAT BRANDS NEED TO **STAY RELEVANT**

My personal RQ goals for 2024 are to learn to crochet and learn to speak Zulu, a widely-spoken African language. I've started beginners' classes in both and I'll keep you posted!

Professionally my RQ goal for 2024 is to launch our online course academy called *She Ignites*. It's an online learning platform for female leadership programmes where women find courses to advance their careers. We've never done this before, so it's been a great challenge. Our market has typically been B2B (Business to Business) and now we're launching a B2C (Business to Consumer) model, alongside our B2B existing offering. It's one of the most exciting and nerve-wracking things I've ever done in my career.

I'm noticing how challenged myself and my team feel every day. We're leaning into the challenge. I have a life philosophy that has helped me summon courage and do challenging things, which I learned when I ran the New York marathon in 2011. I had never run a marathon before (or since). I thought if I was going to kill myself then let me do it in style in New York, one of my favourite cities in the world. It was honestly one of the best days of my life, and I learned a valuable lesson. I can tackle difficult things.

Break it down!

The New York marathon is 26,2 miles so I decided to break it down into 26 x 1 mile races. After each mile there is a watering station so I'd stop and take a break, sip water or Coke, take a photo, re-group and start with the next mile.

This philosophy has worked well in the conquering of my RQ goals – break them down into smaller chunks and move forward, bravely!

"The introverted mind is rich with ideas and creativity. Staying relevant helps those ideas reach and resonate with the right audiences."

Marti Olsen Laney

WHAT CAN INTROVERTS DO TO INCREASE THEIR RQ?

1. Feel the fear and do it anyway
Being scared means you're doing the right thing.

2. Commit to life-long learning
Take online courses, attend webinars and read extensively in your field. This ensures you stay up to date with the latest trends, technology and systems. Look for learning formats that suit your more Introverted nature such as self-paced online courses or reading.

3. Leverage your deep thinking
Introverts are generally deep thinkers. Use this to your advantage by diving deep into your world of expertise. Write articles, blog posts or white papers that showcase your deep understanding and unique perspectives. This can help establish you as a thought leader, and also naturally develops your personal brand.

4. Develop a strong online presence
Use social media and professional networking sites like LinkedIn. This will enable you to share your knowledge and insights, connect with peers and stay informed about your industry. These platforms can be excellent ways for Introverts to network and share their expertise on their own terms.

5. Embrace small-scale networking
Instead of large networking events, focus on one-on-one meetings or small groups where deeper, more meaningful connections are possible. Prepare questions and topics in advance to make these interactions more comfortable and productive.

NETWORKING FOR **INTROVERTS**

GREAT BRANDS NEED TO **STAY RELEVANT**

6. Practise public speaking

While this might seem counter-intuitive for Introverts, becoming more comfortable with public speaking can significantly enhance your visibility and relevance. Start small with presentations to small groups or join a Toastmasters Club either in your area or company. This will increase your confidence enormously. Presenting is a learned skill – the more you do it the better you get!

ACTIVITY

Download your RQ goal sheet with the QR code at the beginning of the book.

NETWORKING FOR **INTROVERTS**

CHAPTER 7
YOU CAN'T BE BRAVE IF YOU'RE **NOT WELL**

We've already discussed how the currency of Relevance is Bravery. If you aren't scared by your RQ goals you're not doing them right!

Being brave often requires a reservoir of strength, resilience and the ability to confront challenges head-on. However, when one's wellness

— physical, mental or emotional — is compromised, these resources can be significantly depleted, making acts of bravery much more challenging.

Your physical well-being is foundational to your ability to perform acts that might require bravery. If you are physically unwell, the energy and strength needed to tackle physically demanding challenges can be diminished. If you're not sleeping well, you are unlikely to be able to feel or be brave.

Your brain goes into fight-or-flight mode when it's stressed – using the caveman part of your brain, the amygdala. We are generally not the best versions of ourselves operating in the survival part of our brain – because it's only aim is to keep us alive.

High Performance Model 2024

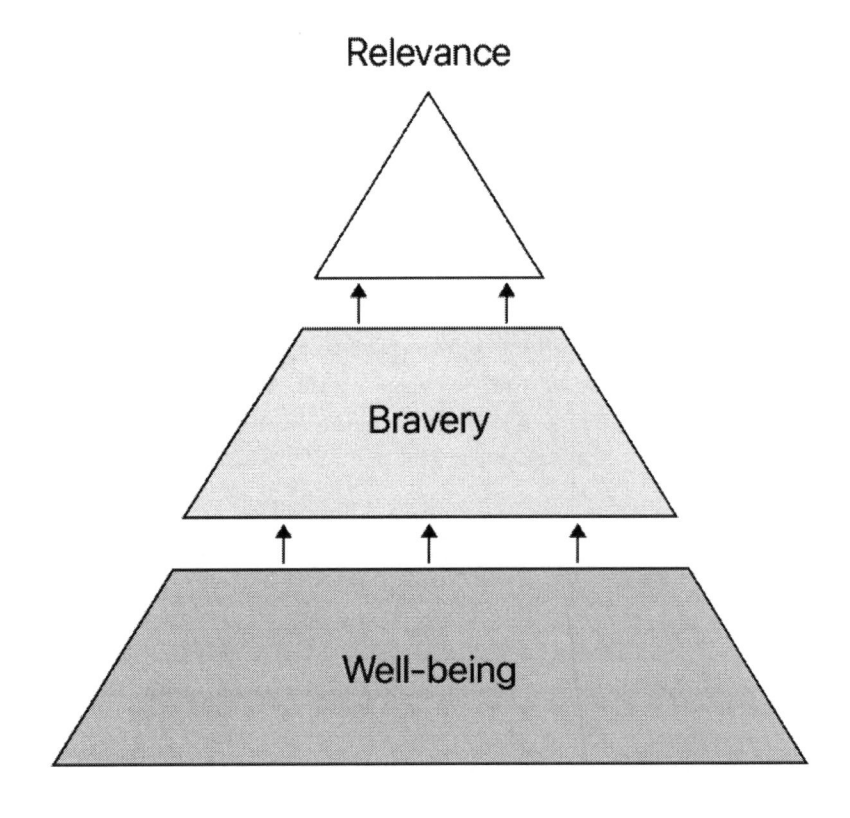

- Relevance
- Bravery
- Well-being

- Helen Nicholson

Advanced and strategic thinking happens in the pre-frontal cortex of our brains. Bravery is an advanced high-level function. We are unable to access the pre-frontal cortex when we're stressed because it's in self- preservation mode.

Mental well-being also plays a crucial role in bravery. Courage often demands a clear mind, the ability to assess risks and the mental strength to face potential fears. Mental health issues, such as anxiety or depression, can cloud judgment, amplify fears, and decrease the capacity to manage stress, thereby affecting one's ability to exhibit bravery.

Overall well-being provides the energy, clarity, and stability required to navigate through difficult circumstances with courage. Without it, the effort to act bravely can become significantly more challenging.

I think this model summarises the link between well-being, bravery, relevancy and high performance very well:
- You Can't Be Brave if you're not well
- Bravery is the currency of Relevance
- Relevance leads to High Performance

What do Introverts have to learn about bravery and their well-being?

Introverts, like everyone else, face unique challenges when it comes to bravery and their well-being. Given their natural inclination towards introspection and a preference for solitary activities or small group interactions, Introverts may approach situations requiring bravery quite differently to Extroverts. Here are several key insights and strategies that can help introverts navigate their paths to bravery and wellbeing:

"Quiet people have the loudest minds. It takes bravery to share that inner world with others."

Stephen Hawking

1. Understanding Personal Boundaries

Introverts need to be mindful of their energy levels and personal boundaries. Engaging in activities that require bravery often means stepping out of one's comfort zone, which can be energy-depleting for Introverts. Learning to recognise and respect personal limits is crucial in maintaining well-being, while also being open to growth and new experiences.

2. Small Steps Lead to Big Leaps

For Introverts, the act of bravery doesn't have to be a grand gesture. Small acts of courage, like speaking up during a meeting, attending social events or trying new activities, can significantly contribute to personal growth. These steps can build resilience and confidence, making larger challenges feel more achievable.

3. Leveraging Inner Strengths

Introverts possess a rich inner world, with deep thoughts and the ability to reflect profoundly on experiences. These qualities can be strengths when facing challenging situations. For instance, Introverts can use their capacity for deep thought to plan and prepare for situations that might require bravery, turning introspection into a strategic advantage.

4. Finding Comfort in Solitude

Solitude is often where Introverts recharge and find peace. Embracing this need, rather than seeing it as a limitation can be empowering. Solitude can also be a space for introspection about what bravery means to them personally, allowing Introverts to approach challenges in a way that aligns with their values and strengths.

"Introverts, by staying relevant, can demonstrate that quiet leadership and innovation are just as powerful as any extroverted approach."

Adam Grant

5. Practicing Self-Compassion

Introverts, especially those who are highly self-reflective, may be hard on themselves for feeling fearful or hesitant. Practising self-compassion is essential, recognising that bravery is not about the absence of fear but acting despite it. Self-compassion involves acknowledging one's feelings, treating oneself with kindness and understanding that challenges are part of growth.

6. Seeking Supportive Relationships

While Introverts might prefer a smaller circle of close, meaningful relationships, these connections can be a source of strength and encouragement. Sharing fears and aspirations with trusted friends or mentors can provide Introverts with the support they need to face challenges bravely.

Bravery for Introverts involves finding the balance between respecting their natural inclinations and challenging themselves to grow. By understanding and leveraging their unique strengths, practising self- compassion and taking incremental steps toward their goals, Introverts can navigate the path to bravery in a way that preserves and enhances their well-being.

NETWORKING FOR **INTROVERTS**

CHAPTER 8
BECOME A BETTER **STORYTELLER**

During the research for all my books, I've learned that becoming a better storyteller is one of the best ways to become more impactful in your influence and presence.

Story is what the brain does. It is a "story processor," writes psychologist Professor Jonathan Haidt, not "a logic processor." Stories emerge from human minds as naturally as breath emerges from human lips. You don't have to be a genius to master it – in fact, you're already doing it. This chapter gives you the structure required to master the art of storytelling.

A widely recommended and versatile storytelling structure is the "Three-Act Structure," which is fundamental in most storytelling structures and has been used in plays, novels, movies, short stories and the best PowerPoint presentations.

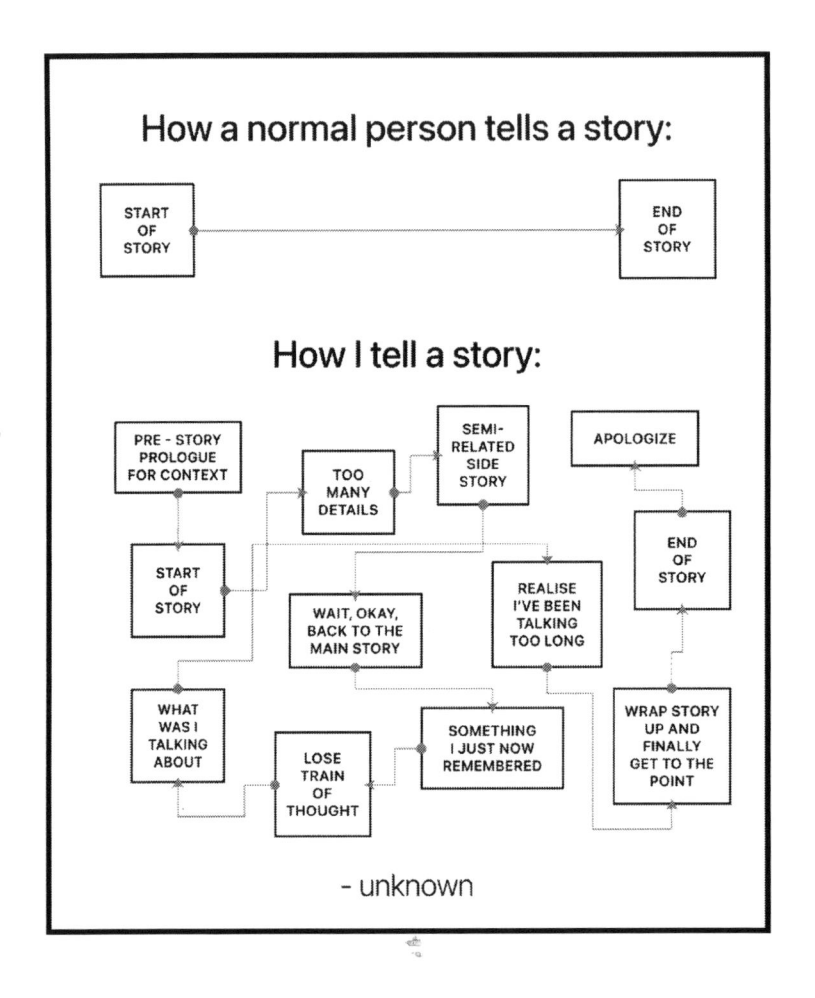

NETWORKING FOR **INTROVERTS**

How a normal person tells a story:

START OF STORY ────────────── END OF STORY

How I tell a story:

- START OF STORY
- PRE-STORY PROLOGUE FOR CONTEXT
- TOO MANY DETAILS
- SEMI-RELATED SIDE STORY
- WAIT, OKAY, BACK TO THE MAIN STORY
- REALISE I'VE BEEN TALKING TOO LONG
- APOLOGIZE
- WHAT WAS I TALKING ABOUT
- LOSE TRAIN OF THOUGHT
- SOMETHING I JUST NOW REMEMBERED
- WRAP STORY UP AND FINALLY GET TO THE POINT
- END OF STORY

– unknown

This structure provides a straightforward framework that helps organise a story's beginning, middle, and end in a way that's compelling and easy for the audience to follow. Here's a breakdown:

Storytelling Structure:
Act 1: Set-up

Introduction: Introduce the main characters, setting and the story's world. Establish the normal state of affairs for your protagonist.

Inciting Incident: Present an event that disrupts the status quo. This incident propels your protagonist into the main conflict or quest of the story.

Point of No Return: Conclude the first act with a decisive event that makes the protagonist's journey and the ensuing confrontation inevitable.

Act 2: Confrontation

Rising Action: The protagonist faces obstacles, challenges, and further complications. This is where secondary characters, sub-plots and additional conflicts are developed.

Midpoint: A key event occurs that changes the protagonist's approach to solving their obstacles or problems. It often shifts the story's direction and reveals new information.

Crisis: The protagonist faces their biggest challenge yet, leading to the lowest point in their journey. This moment tests their resolve and commitment to their goal.

"Introverts have a natural ability to create vivid, detailed stories, because they spend so much time observing and reflecting on their experiences."

Sophia Dembling

Act 3: Resolution

>**Climax:** The story's tension reaches its peak. The protagonist confronts the main conflict head-on and their goal is either achieved or definitively thwarted.
>
>**Failing Action:** The immediate consequences of the climax are dealt with. Loose ends start to tie up.
>
>**Resolution:** The story concludes with a return to a new normal, where the outcomes of the protagonist's journey are evident. This section resolves any remaining sub-plots and shows how the characters have changed.

This structure is popular because it mirrors the natural arc of many human experiences — setting out on a journey, facing and overcoming challenges and then returning home changed.

It helps create a satisfying narrative experience for the people you're speaking to by building anticipation, developing tension and then providing resolution.

I tell a tooth fairy story to open my Mindful Resilience presentation, and I've broken it down into the Three-Act structure as an example of good verbal storytelling.

"Storytelling is about connecting with people on an emotional level. Introverts excel at this because they listen deeply and empathize with others."

Jennifer Kahnweiler

I received coaching on delivering this message, and found that it landed much more powerfully using the Three-Act structure.

Storytelling - Real-life Example:
Act 1: Set-up

> **Introduction:** The story starts with the introduction of the main characters — myself and my eight-year-old twins. The setting is my home, a place where childhood beliefs like the tooth fairy are alive and vibrant. The twins, having lost their molar teeth on that day, are filled with excitement and anticipation for the tooth fairy's visit.
>
> **Inciting Incident:** The excitement of the twins sets the stage for the story's central conflict. Their belief in the tooth fairy, represented by their lost teeth placed in their slippers, is the emotional investment that draws the audience in.
>
> **Point of No Return:** The next morning, when the twins found their teeth still in their slippers with no money left in exchange, marks the point of no return.

The disappointment is palpable, but it's my forgetfulness that propels the story into its next phase, highlighting the underlying issue of living an unmindful life.

Act 2: Confrontation

> **Rising Action:** My repeated forgetfulness over the next three days escalates the tension. Each morning that the twins find their teeth still in their slippers, anticipation and excitement turns into confusion and disappointment, reflecting the growing problem.

"The quieter you become, the more you can hear. Introverts have a deep reservoir of stories waiting to be told."

Ram Dass

Midpoint: My forgetfulness reaches the point where the narrative takes a turn — this is not just about a missed tooth fairy visit but a reflection of a larger issue in my life, indicating a disconnect from the present and the important moments in my children's lives.

Crisis: The crisis comes to a head when Sabrina, one of the twins, confronts me directly. This confrontation — "Mommy, I don't believe in the tooth fairy anymore" — is the emotional climax of the conflict, starkly highlighting the impact of my actions (or lack thereof).

Act 3: Resolution

Climax: Sabrina's statement acts as the story's climax. It's not just about the loss of belief in a childhood fantasy but a poignant moment of realisation for me. This moment of confrontation is where the main theme of the story — mindfulness and presence in life — is most strongly felt.

Failing Action: The immediate aftermath of Sabrina's realisation and my own acknowledgment of the issue begin to resolve the story's tension. It's understood that something has to change.

Resolution: The resolution of my story isn't just the correction of a single mistake but a fundamental shift in my approach to life. The realisation that I wasn't living a mindful, present life acts as the catalyst for change, promising a future where there are fewer moments of disconnect.

My story illustrates how everyday moments and the realisations that result from them can lead to profound personal growth.

"*Introverts show their bravery not by being the loudest in the room, but by being the most thoughtful, the most reflective, and the most prepared.*"

Jennifer Kahnweiler

It's a relatable story as many parents have forgotten key moments, and it also reveals my vulnerability. It emphasises the importance of being present and mindful for the small yet significant moments in life.

The key to telling better stories is to practise them in front of the mirror and practise them on your family and friends, gradually gaining the confidence to tell the story at a cocktail party or a work function.

A good storytelling structure for introducing yourself can follow a similar format:

The Set-up
Start by providing some context about who you are and where you're from. This could include your name, hometown, family background, education or career path. Set the scene.

Example: "My name is Sarah, and I grew up in a small town in Vermont called Woodstock..."

The Pivotal Moment
Then, share a specific pivotal moment, experience or realisation that shaped who you are today. This is the "hook" that pulls the listener into your story.

Example: "When I was 12, my family took a trip to Italy that sparked my love of travel and different cultures..."

The Obstacle/Challenge
What obstacle or challenge did you face related to this experience? How did you approach or overcome it? This adds drama and depth.

Example: "As a shy kid, I was nervous about getting lost or not knowing the language. But I quickly learned how to use gestures and a phrasebook..."

"Introverts make great storytellers because they are keen observers and deep thinkers, always finding meaning in the world around them."

Susan Cain

The Insight/Growth
Explain how this pivotal moment impacted your perspective, values or goals. What did you learn about yourself?

Example: "That trip taught me to step out of my comfort zone and that amazing things happen when you open yourself up to new experiences..."

The Current Truth/ Changed Reality
Circle back to who you are now as a result of that experience. How does it connect to why you're here today?

Example: "...So now, whether I'm traveling for work or pleasure, I always make sure to immerse myself in the local culture."

By structuring your introduction as a mini-story hitting those key points, you share something memorable and insightful about yourself in an engaging way.

As an Introvert, your preference for introspection and deep thinking can actually be advantageous for storytelling. Here are some steps and tips that can help you become a better storyteller:

1. Observe and Listen
Observe life around you. Real-life experiences, people's behaviours and the natural world are great sources of inspiration.
Listen to other storytellers. Whether it's through podcasts, audiobooks, or conversations, notice how effective storytellers structure their stories and engage their audience.

"Introverts, with their attention to detail and introspective nature, can turn the simplest of experiences into captivating stories."

Beth Buelow

2. Read Widely

Expand your reading. Reading a variety of genres and styles can introduce you to different storytelling techniques and narrative structures.

Analyse stories. Pay attention to how stories are built — take note of the introduction, build-up, climax and resolution.

3. Practise Writing

Start writing your stories. Writing helps to clarify your thoughts and develop your voice.

Keep a journal. This can be a rich source of material for your stories. Reflect on your experiences and feelings.

4. Start Small

Share stories informally. Begin by telling short stories to friends or family in a comfortable setting.

Practice storytelling in your mind. Visualise telling a story and how you might phrase it or emphasise certain points.

5. Embrace Your Unique Perspective

Use your introspection. Your inner life as an Introvert can provide deep insights and unique angles on common themes.

Be authentic. Authenticity resonates with people. Don't be afraid to show vulnerability in your stories.

6. Get Feedback

Seek constructive criticism. Ask friends, family, or fellow storytellers for feedback on how you can improve.

Be open to learning. Each piece of feedback is an opportunity to grow.

NETWORKING FOR **INTROVERTS**

"I think the best way to get over the anxiety of networking is to reframe it in your mind. Think of it as just having a conversation with a friend."

Dorie Clark

7. Practise, Practise, Practise

Tell stories often. The more you tell stories, the more comfortable you'll become.

Reflect on your performances. Think about what worked and what didn't, and why.

8. Use Technology to Your Advantage

Record yourself. Listening to recordings of your storytelling can highlight areas for improvement.

Remember, storytelling is a skill that improves with time and practice. As an Introvert, you have a unique viewpoint and depth of thought that can make your stories deeply resonant and compelling. Embrace your individuality and use it to enrich your storytelling.

PART 1
ACTION PLAN

My biggest wish for you as you complete this first part Brand (YOU) Pty Ltd of the book is to go out and:

1. Realise how the neuroscience of being an Introvert affects the way you respond to stimuli.
2. Package your brand in a mindful intentional way, taking into account your strengths.
3. Conduct an energy audit to see where you are on the Career Sweet Spot grid.
4. Find out what your Personal Branding coffee stain is and fix it. You are more than your coffee stain!
4. Develop RQ (Relevancy Quotient) goals both personally and professionally every year, so your brand always grows and stays relevant.
5. You can't be Brave if you're not well!

SUMMARY OF ACTIVITIES

- Assessment to find out if you are an Introvert, Extrovert or Ambivert
- Energy Audit tracker
- Key Achievements tracker
- Coffee Stain tracker
- RQ goal sheet

PART 2
MASTER THE ART OF
NETWORKING

CHAPTER 9
THE TOP **CHARACTERISTICS** OF THE **BEST NETWORKERS**

Personal Branding is the Why and Networking is the How! If you understand fundamentally who you are as an Introvert, you lean into your strengths and stop focusing on your weaknesses, fix your coffee stain and retain relevance through establishing regular Relevancy RQ goals both personally and professionally. Then you've done a great job at starting to package your value.

Now it's time to communicate your packaged value to your target market/audience through your network.

There are three characteristics of the best networkers based on my research. They:
1. Operate from a spirit of abundance;
2. Are curious; and
3. Have presence.

"We make a living by what we get, but we make a life by what we give."

Winston Churchill

THE TOP **CHARACTERISTICS** OF THE **BEST NETWORKERS**

Let's unpack them individually:

1. The best networkers have an abundance mentality

They operate with an open hand – they think, "What can I give, not what can I take." They are generous with their resources – time, knowledge, money, love and support.

It's the one characteristic that came up in every single interview I conducted with the best networkers for my last book, *Networking: How to get your black book in business success.* The value system of operating from a spirit of abundance cuts across Introversion, Extroversion, industries, ages and genders.

The best networkers are Givers in my experience. I'm not talking about giving and giving and giving and getting nothing in return. There is a spirit of reciprocity underlying all networking. I believe in giving first - I will give at least three to four times to a new relationship. If I receive nothing in return, then I'd stop giving. I'd know then that I'm dealing with a taker – and generally Givers and Takers are not destined to have long- lasting networking relationships. They're more transactional in nature and don't last long.

On the other hand, a Giver and a Giver relationship can last an entire career and lifetime, as they both share common values.

Adam Grant, one of my favourite authors and social scientists believes in his ground-breaking book, *Give and Take*, that success depends heavily on how we approach our interactions with other people. Every time we interact with another person at work, we have a decision to make: Do we try to claim as much value as we can, or contribute value without worrying about what we receive in return.

"You can have everything in life you want, if you will just help other people get what they want."

Zig Ziglar

THE TOP **CHARACTERISTICS** OF THE **BEST NETWORKERS**

Grant, in his book, expands on my definition of Givers and Takers. He states that social scientists have discovered that people differ dramatically in their preferences for reciprocity – their desired mix of giving and taking.

Takers have a distinctive signature: they like to get more than they give. They tilt reciprocity in their favour, putting their own interests first. Takers believe in a competitive dog-eat-dog world. They feel that to succeed, they need to be better than others. To prove their competence, they self-promote and make sure they get plenty of credit for their efforts. Garden variety Takers aren't cruel or cut-throat, they're just cautious and self-protective. "If I don't look out for myself first," Takers think, "then no-one will."

If you're a Giver at work, you strive to be generous in sharing your time, energy, knowledge, skills, ideas and connections with other people who can benefit from them. You don't focus on what you can get in return.

You may think that to be a Giver at work you need to be Mother Teresa or Mahatma Gandhi, but being a Giver doesn't require extraordinary acts of sacrifice. It just involves a focus on acting in the interests of others, such as giving help, providing mentoring, sharing credit or making connections with others.

Outside work, this behaviour is quite common. According to research led by Yale psychologist, Margaret Clarke, most people like to act like Givers in their close relationships. In marriages and friendships, we contribute whenever we can without keeping score.

"It's easier to win if everybody wants you to win. If you don't make enemies out there, it's so much easier to succeed."

Unknown

THE TOP **CHARACTERISTICS** OF THE **BEST NETWORKERS**

If I asked you to guess who's the most likely to end up at the top of the success ladder, would you choose a Giver or a Taker?

Many people have a belief system that "the good girl/guy finishes last" – and that good girl/guy is often an Introvert.

When more than six hundred medical students in Belgium were studied, the students with the lowest marks, had unusually high scores on Giver statements like:
"I love to help others" and
"I actively see where I can add the most value."

The Givers in the study went out of their way to help their peers study, sharing what they already knew to the detriment of their own learning. On the face of this data it appears that Givers are just too caring, too trusting and too willing to sacrifice their own interests for the benefit of others.

Adam Grant then discovered a surprising pattern: Givers do gain (in the end that is). What is unique about the success of Givers is that it spreads and cascades. When Takers win, there's usually someone else who loses. Research shows that people tend to envy successful Takers and look for ways to bring them down a notch. In contrast, when Givers win, people are rooting for them and supporting them, rather than gunning for them.

A famous Introvert, Abraham Lincoln, was determined to put the good of the nation above his own ego. When he won the presidency in 1860, he invited the three candidates whom he defeated for the Republican nomination to become his Secretary of State, Secretary of the Treasury and Attorney General.

"No one has ever become poor by giving."

Anne Frank

THE TOP **CHARACTERISTICS** OF THE **BEST NETWORKERS**

Historian Doris Goodwin documents how unusual Lincoln's cabinet was:

"Every member of the administration was better known, better educated and more experienced in public life than Lincoln. Their presence in the cabinet might have threatened to eclipse Abraham Lincoln, the obscure prairie lawyer."

In Lincoln's position, a Taker might have preferred to protect his ego and power by inviting "yes men" to join him. Yet Lincoln invited his bitter competitors instead.

If politics can be fertile ground for Givers, it's possible that Givers can succeed in any job. The most important thing when determining the effectiveness of giving is the nature of the exchange. In purely zero-sum situations and win-lose interactions, giving rarely pays off. However, most of life isn't zero-sum and on balance, people who choose giving as their primary reciprocity style end up reaping rewards.

It takes time for Givers to build goodwill and trust, but eventually they establish reputations and relationships that enhance their success. The Giver advantage grows over time.

If we go back to the Belgian medical students, in the first year the Givers were finishing last. By the second year, the Givers had closed the gap. They were now significantly outperforming their peers.

By the sixth year, the Givers were earning substantially higher grades.

Nothing about the Givers had changed but their programme did. As students passed through medical school they moved from theoretical classes into clinical rotations, internships and patient care. The further

"My greatest strength as a consultant is to be ignorant and ask a few questions."

Peter Drucker

THE TOP CHARACTERISTICS OF THE BEST NETWORKERS

they advanced, the more their success depended on teamwork and service. As the structure of class work shifted, the Givers benefitted from their natural tendencies to collaborate effectively with other medical professionals and express concern to patients. They will think in the relationship space!

The Giver advantage is not limited to medicine. Steve Jones, the award- winning former CEO of one Australia's largest banks, wanted to know what made financial advisors successful. His team studied key factors such as financial expertise and effort. But the "single most influential factor" was whether the financial advisor had the clients' best interests at heart, above the company's and even their own. It was one of Joneses' top three priorities to get that value instilled and demonstrate that it's in everybody's interests to treat clients that way.

2. Great networkers are curious

This is where Introverts come into their own, as 90% of the Introverts I interviewed for this book rated their curiosity as over 75%.

A great networker's secret weapon is curiosity.

Research indicates that on average, curiosity increases at about 12 years of age. But by the age of 30, curiosity drops off. However, Introverts curiousity leads to learning. Life long curiousity results in life long learning! Keep their curiosity growing and it becomes their superpower.

"The best way to find yourself is to lose yourself in the service of others."

Mahatma Gandhi

THE TOP **CHARACTERISTICS** OF THE **BEST NETWORKERS**

How to take your curiosity to the next level:

1. **Ask powerful questions.**
   Good questions are the currency of curiosity. Asking powerful questions is the first step in showing people that you are:
   - Willing to explore diverse points of view
   - Aware that your way isn't always the best way
   - Interested in what and how the other person thinks

   Be specific when you ask questions. Don't simply ask, "How was the conference?" Instead, be specific "I really enjoyed the presentation on Mindfulness – what was your biggest takeaway?"

   Use words like "How", "What" and "Tell me about" to set up powerful questions.
   - How did you reach that conclusion?
   - Take me through the key areas?
   - What do you see as the next steps?
   - What are your other options?

2. **Really listen and make people feel heard.**
   My mother used to say to us growing up, "There's a reason we have two ears and one mouth." We need to use our ears twice the amount of time we use our mouths.

   Introverts are really good at this. They listen deeply and also observe the nuances of the other person. I think a good listening ratio is 60% listening and 40% talking. Introverts just need to ensure they are heard as well, and this is where telling better stories comes in (more about that in Chapter Eight) People's brains are wired to hear stories so you become more memorable when you tell good stories.

"Being Heard is so close to being loved, that for the average person they are almost indistinguishable."

David Augsberger

THE TOP **CHARACTERISTICS** OF THE **BEST NETWORKERS**

In his book, *"The Speed of Trust: the One thing that Changes Everything"*, Stephen Covey says it well: "Listen before you speak. Understand. Diagnose. Listen with your ears, your eyes and your heart."

When you're on your phone and not listening to the person you're with, you come across as distracted. The message you're sending the other person is, "You're not important." Interrupting also implies that you're not really listening.

Oprah said in all the time hosting her talk show, the greatest realisation was that the biggest need for human beings is the need to feel heard. Here are some ways you can make someone feel heard:
- Making eye contact and nodding
- Reflecting back, "So what I'm hearing you say is xxxx. Is that correct?"
- Asking powerful follow-up questions that show you were paying attention and truly hearing what the person has to say.

3. Great networkers have presence
Presence is probably the one characteristic Introverts battle with most.

Ways to increase your presence:
Start off with your body language:

- **Maintain good eye contact**
  This shows you're engaged and interested. You don't need to stare, just try and maintain natural eye contact while listening and speaking.

"The cure for boredom is curiosity. There is no cure for curiosity."

Dorothy Parker.

THE TOP CHARACTERISTICS OF THE BEST NETWORKERS

- **Work on your posture**
  Stand or sit up straight with your shoulders back. Good posture conveys confidence and openness. Avoid crossing your arms or legs in a way that may come across as defensive or closed off.

- **Use open gesture**
  Use your hands to express yourself when speaking but keep your gestures open and inclusive rather than closed or small. This doesn't mean you have to gesture a lot if that's not natural for you, but being more expressive can make you seem more approachable and dynamic. I always advise Introverts to hold onto something in meetings, such as a pen, or a glass at cocktail parties, as that often makes open gestures feel more comfortable. Make sure not to over do it as it can be distracting.

- **Smile genuinely**
  As you walk into a meeting, conference or presentation – smile! A genuine smile makes you appear more approachable and friendly. It also helps to ease your own nervousness in social situations.

- **Work on your walking**
  Your walk can say a lot about your confidence. Practise walking with a purpose, with your head held high, making moderate eye contact with people as you pass. Make sure to be relaxed, so you don't appear aggressive.

NETWORKING FOR **INTROVERTS**

"There is a reason we have two ears and one mouth."

My Mom

THE TOP **CHARACTERISTICS** OF THE **BEST NETWORKERS**

- **Use space wisely**
  When speaking in a group or meeting, standing up (if appropriate) will increase your presence and make you more visible.

  If sitting, whenever you have something to say, lean forward and bullet point the points you want to convey. Say, "I have two or three points that I believe are relevant to this meeting." Make the points, then lean back and say "What's our action plan to deal with these issues?" This communication technique dramatically increases people's perception of you – you are seen as powerful, clear and influential.

ACTIVITY

Take the Curiosity Assessment quiz by downloading it from the QR code at the beginning of the book.

CHAPTER 10
WHO ARE THE **POWER BROKERS** IN NETWORKS?

The people in a network are not equal in terms of their influence and power. There are certain individuals or groups of people who are more important than others. As well as your personal board of directors (more about them later in the chapter) there are important groups of people called Connectors and Mavens.

CONNECTORS AND MAVENS

Connectors

I believe Connectors play an important role in Introverts' networks as they become the unofficial PR agent of your personal brand, if managed correctly.

Connectors are people who know people. If you know 50 people a connector will know 500 people. They are exponentially connected. Connectors have a wide network and excel at bringing people together and connecting the people in their networks.

Paul Revere & William Dawes

- Harvard Business Review, 2005

WHO ARE THE **POWER BROKERS** IN **NETWORKS?**

Connectors often have diverse networks - they know a large number of people across different social, cultural and professional circles. They have a unique and natural ability to make connections between people who otherwise might not ordinarily have met.

Connectors are the VIPs of networking because they facilitate the spread of information by making introductions and linking people who can benefit from knowing each other.

They enjoy meeting new people and are typically very sociable and outgoing.

There is a great story about Connectors in action during the American War of Independence in 1775. The British were about to invade America and two men were sent out on a dark and stormy night to spread the news, "The British are coming", and to gather the army. These men were Paul Revere and William Dawes. Paul Revere was a Connector and William Dawes was not.

Paul Revere, knowing that he only had 24 hours, galloped from town-to-town on his horse. He didn't have time to speak to every single person. As a Connector he instinctively knew that he needed to find out who the Connectors were in each small town, tell them and they would spread the word to everyone else.

He was effectively able to mobilise the troops.

William Dawes, the non-Connector, made the classic networking mistake of treating everyone as equal. He spent his 24 hours knocking on individual doors and he wasn't able to galvanise an army or effectively spread the word.

The Networks of Paul Revere & William Dawes

Paul Revere   William Dawes

- Harvard Business Review, 2005

WHO ARE THE **POWER BROKERS** IN **NETWORKS?**

Paul Revere later stood for office in the American government and had a cigarette brand named after him.

No-one heard of William Dawes again.

I'm fascinated by Connectors and often try to identify whether someone is a Connector by asking a few questions. If you arrive at a function at the same time as another person and you realise you're both driving the same car, a good technique to find out if they're a Connector is to say, "I see we're driving the same brand of car, where do you suggest I get it serviced?" A Connector will immediately take out their phone and connect you to their favourite car dealership/repair shop. The giveaway line is, "Tell them I sent you." Connectors do this all the time and I know if I went to the car dealership the Connector referred me to, that Connector has probably referred many people to them. They do it instinctively!

Once Introverts identify the Connectors in their network they need to leverage these relationships in two very specific ways:

1. Keep in regular contact with your Connectors – at least once every three months. When I interviewed Connectors for my last book, a strong theme that emerged was that they are out-of-sight, out-of-mind people. You have their 100% attention in a one-on-one situation and their mind will be flipping through a mental Rolodex as to who they can connect you to, based on what you need.

They are often not good at following up, so you may need to nudge that process along. Many of the Connectors in my research confessed that once they've left the meeting, then you're gone from their thoughts. They're onto the next interaction.

"Introverts bring a unique value as connectors and mavens, using their deep understanding and empathy to create and share meaningful connections."

William Arruda

WHO ARE THE **POWER BROKERS** IN **NETWORKS?**

For this reason it's important to prepare for these meetings, and try to get a commitment or information from them during the meeting.

I've built our business, The Networking Company, by having regular contact with the Connectors in my network. I can track revenue dips in our business when I'm not in regular contact with my Connectors. They are the unofficial marketing agents for you or your business brand. If a Connector buys into you and your Personal Brand, then they will spread the word about you and your contributions.

2. In my experience, **Connectors prefer direct contact.** They are often on the phone as people are always calling them asking for recommendations. They will be busy helping other people solve their problems but they are not having long catch-up telephonic chats. Also, they are generally not great at following up on email.

Connectors are the people you need to meet for in person- coffees, lunches, drinks and breakfasts. They will assist in building a very powerful Personal Brand – if you stay in contact and see them regularly face-to-face.

Mavens
Mavens are the information specialists. They are the people who accumulate knowledge and understand how to share it with others. Mavens often have in-depth knowledge about certain products, trends or industries, and are driven by the desire to solve problems and share insights. Mavens are trusted sources of information and advice. Their recommendations can significantly influence the opinions and

NETWORKING FOR **INTROVERTS**

"*Introverts excel as connectors because they listen more than they speak, understanding others' needs and facilitating meaningful connections.*"

Laurie Helgoe

behaviours of their social circles.

Many foodies are Mavens.
Many technology gurus are Mavens.
Many Mavens are influencers on social media.

KEY DIFFERENCES BETWEEN CONNECTORS AND MAVENS

1. Connectors will bridge the gaps between different social groups in a network, while Mavens can provide the content of the connections. Connectors introduce people to each other, whereas mavens introduce people to new information or ideas.

2. Type of influence: Connectors influence through their social connections and the breadth of their network. Mavens influence through their knowledge, expertise and the trust people place in their recommendations.

3. Motivation: Connectors are driven by the sheer joy of social interaction and making connections. I'm a Connector and I completely identify with this – I love introducing people who go on to do great things together.
Professional matchmakers and recruitment consultants have made careers of connecting people. Connecting is a vital part of their work. Mavens are motivated by the desire to share information and help others make informed choices.

Both Connectors and Mavens play critical roles in how information and ideas spread through networks, but they do so in very different ways.

"Introverts are natural mavens, absorbing information and sharing it with those who can benefit the most, creating a ripple effect of knowledge."

Marti Olsen Laney

WHO ARE THE POWER BROKERS IN NETWORKS?

The same person can be both a Connector and a Maven which makes them very powerful in a network.

ARE INTROVERTS BETTER CONNECTORS OR MAVENS?

Introverts can be great Connectors and Mavens but their natural tendencies and strengths may make them more naturally inclined towards the role of Mavens. Here's why:

Introverts as Mavens

1. Depth of Knowledge
Introverts often prefer deep dives into subjects of interest, accumulating a wealth of information. This aligns with the Maven's role of being an information specialist who enjoys sharing knowledge with others to help them make better decisions.

2. Thoughtful communication
Introverts typically prefer meaningful one-on-one conversations where they can discuss topics at length. This preference for thoughtful communication makes them well-suited to the Maven's role, where sharing detailed and useful information is key.

3. Trusted advice
Due to their inclination towards authenticity and depth in relationships, Introverts can become trusted sources of information within their networks. People often turn to them for advice and insights, recognising their expertise in specific areas.

NETWORKING FOR **INTROVERTS**

WHAT YOU SAID

HOW MUCH I READ INTO IT

@introvertmemes

WHO ARE THE **POWER BROKERS** IN **NETWORKS?**

4. Listening skills
Introverts are excellent listeners, a trait that serves Mavens well. Being a good listener helps them understand exactly what information others might find helpful or interesting, allowing them to tailor their advice and recommendations effectively.

INTROVERTS AS CONNECTORS

While Introverts might naturally gravitate towards being Mavens, they can also be effective Connectors by leveraging their strengths in different ways:

1. Quality over quantity
Introverts may have smaller networks but their relationships are often deeper. They can act as Connectors within these close-knit circles, introducing people who may genuinely benefit from knowing each other.

2. Selective socialising
When Introverts choose to engage socially, they can be very intentional about it. They might not connect people across vast networks like extroverted Connectors, but they can still be strategic in making meaningful connections.

3. Social networks
The rise of social media and online communities has made it easier for Introverts to connect with others without the need for face-to-face interactions.

YOU'RE ONLY AS GOOD AS WHO YOU SURROUND YOURSELF WITH

The 12 roles in your Personal Boardroom

Information roles
provide new knowledge, insights and ideas

Customer voice	Expert
Inspirer	Navigator

Power roles
provide access to people and resource and get things done

Customer voice	Expert
Inspirer	Navigator

Development roles
provide feedback, challenge, courage and balance

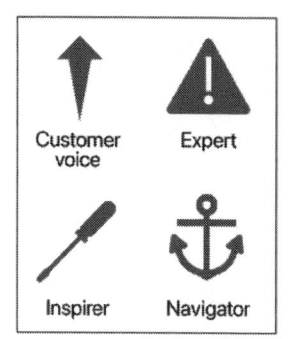

Customer voice	Expert
Inspirer	Navigator

- The Personal Boardroom

WHO ARE THE **POWER BROKERS** IN **NETWORKS?**

Introverts can use these platforms to build networks and connect people from different areas of their lives.

With their deep understanding of subjects, thoughtful communication style and authentic relationships, Introverts can also be effective Connectors, albeit in a more focused and deliberate manner.

The Personal Boardroom

The Personal Boardroom methodology is a powerful tool for professional development and networking. It helps people identify key roles within their network that can support them in achieving their career goals.

The Power roles are the most helpful in networking. Understanding the roles of:
- Unlocker
- Sponsor
- Influencer
- and Connector

within this framework can provide valuable insights into managing and expanding your professional relationships effectively.

Here's a brief description of each role:

Unlocker

An Unlocker is someone who provides you with new opportunities that were previously inaccessible. They can unlock doors to new projects, roles, or industries by leveraging their position, knowledge, or network. Unlockers believe in your potential to succeed in new arenas, and are instrumental in facilitating your entry into spaces where you can grow and excel.

"You are the average of the five people you spend the most time with."

Jim Rohn

WHO ARE THE **POWER BROKERS** IN **NETWORKS?**

Sponsor
A Sponsor goes beyond mere advocacy. They invest in your success and take a proactive role in advancing your career. A Sponsor talks about you when you're not in the room, recommends you for opportunities and puts their reputation on the line for you. They ensure you are considered for promotions, challenging projects, and valuable networking circles. Sponsors are crucial for visibility and career advancement within and outside your current organisation.

Influencer
An Influencer is someone with the power to sway decisions and opinions within your industry or organisation. They may not have a direct stake in your career but their endorsement or advice can significantly impact your professional journey. Influencers have a broad network and a strong reputation, making their support valuable for gaining credibility, validation or broadening your reach.

Connector
A Connector is a master networker who introduces you to others in their extensive network, helping you expand your professional circle. Connectors see the potential in creating relationships and are keen on linking people with mutual interests or complementary goals.

They help you navigate through your career and connect with individuals who can be instrumental in your growth, providing access to resources, knowledge, and opportunities that you might not have had access to on your own.

Each of these roles plays a unique and crucial part in your professional development. By identifying and nurturing relationships with individuals who can serve as Unlockers, Sponsors, Influencers and Connectors, you can strategically navigate your career path with a network that enhances your growth, visibility, and opportunities.

"No one succeeds alone. Surround yourself with a diverse personal boardroom to unlock your full potential."

Sheryl Sandberg

WHO ARE THE **POWER BROKERS** IN **NETWORKS?**

Here is a brief outline of some of the other roles in your Personal Boardroom. I encourage you to audit your network and see who fills which roles, and where your current gaps are.

INFORMATION ROLES (DIFFERENT CATEGORIES OF MAVENS):

Customer Voice

The Customer Voice is someone who provides you with direct insights and feedback from a customer's perspective. This could be an actual customer, a client or someone who understands the needs and challenges of the market you serve. They help you stay aligned with customer needs and market demands, ensuring that your work remains relevant and impactful.

Expert

An Expert offers you deep knowledge and technical expertise in your field or an area you wish to explore. They are your go-to source for authoritative advice, latest trends, and advanced skills. Experts help you elevate your professional competence and keep you at the forefront of industry developments.

Inspirer An Inspirer is someone who motivates and energises you. They embody qualities, achievements or values that you aspire to, encouraging you to aim higher and pursue your goals with passion. Inspirers can be mentors, leaders in your field or anyone whose story and success drives you to realise your own potential.

"Your network is your net worth. For introverts, having a personal boardroom ensures you are supported, inspired, and connected."

Porter Gale

Navigator
Navigators are individuals who have navigated paths or challenges similar to those you might be facing. They offer guidance, share their experiences and help you find your way through complex situations or decisions. Navigators understand the terrain and can help you avoid pitfalls and identify opportunities.

DEVELOPMENT ROLES
Improver
An Improver provides constructive feedback and challenges you to improve continuously. They are honest and forthright in their assessment, focusing on areas where you can develop. Improvers push you towards excellence, ensuring that you don't become complacent and always strive to enhance your skills and output.

Challenger
A Challenger pushes you out of your comfort zone, and challenges your assumptions and ideas. They force you to reconsider your perspectives and approach problems in new ways. Challengers are crucial for innovation and personal growth, as they prevent you from settling into routine thinking and encourage exploration and creativity.

Nerve-Giver
A Nerve-Giver offers emotional support and confidence, especially in times of risk or uncertainty. They believe in your capabilities and bolster your courage to take bold steps. Nerve-Givers are your cheerleaders, providing the encouragement and morale boost needed to tackle challenging situations or pursue ambitious goals.

WHO ARE THE **POWER BROKERS** IN **NETWORKS?**

Anchor

An Anchor provides emotional and sometimes personal support, keeping you grounded. They remind you of your values, goals and the bigger picture, ensuring you stay true to yourself in your professional pursuits. Anchors are your emotional bedrock, offering stability and perspective during turbulent times.

ACTIVITY

If you are interested in auditing your network using the Beehive Process, then download the audit template using the QR code at the beginning of the book.

NETWORKING FOR **INTROVERTS**

CHAPTER 11
WHAT COMES AROUND **GOES AROUND**

There is a great story about the connection between Al Capone, the infamous American gangster of the 1950s, and Butch O'Hare, who had O'Hare International, Chicago's busiest airport, named after him.

> ***Story 1:***
> Many years ago, Al Caponevirtually owned Chicago. Caponewasn't famous for anything heroic. He was notorious for enmeshing the Windy City in everything from bootlegged booze and prostitution to murder.
> Capone had a lawyer nicknamed "Easy Eddie". He was Capone's lawyer for a good reason. Eddie was very good! In fact, Eddie's skill at legal manoeuvring kept Big Al out of jail for a long time.
> To show his appreciation, Capone paid him very well. Not only was the money big, but Eddie got special dividends. He and his family occupied a fenced-in mansion with live-in help and all of the conveniences of the day.

"Life is an echo. What you send out, comes back. What you sow, you reap. What you give, you get. What you see in others, exists in you."

Zig Ziglar

WHO AWHAT COMES AROUND **GOES AROUND**

The estate was so large that it filled an entire Chicago city block. Eddie lived the high life of the Chicago mob and gave little consideration to the violence that went on around him.

Eddie did have one soft spot, however. He had a son that he loved dearly. Eddie saw to it that his young son had clothes, cars, and a good education. Nothing was withheld. Price was no object.

And, despite his involvement with organised crime, Eddie even tried to teach him right from wrong. Eddie wanted his son to be a better man than him.

Yet, with all his wealth and influence, there were two things he couldn't give his son; he couldn't pass on a good name or be a good example. One day, Easy Eddie reached a difficult decision. Easy Eddie wanted to rectify all the wrongs he had done.

He decided he would go to the authorities and tell the truth about Al "Scarface" Capone, clean up his tarnished name, and offer his son some semblance of integrity. To do this, he would have to testify against the mob, and he knew that the cost would be great. Still, he testified.

Within a year, Easy Eddie's life ended in a blaze of gunfire on a lonely Chicago street. But in his eyes, he had given his son the greatest gift he had to offer, at the greatest price he could ever pay. Police removed from his pockets a rosary, a crucifix, a religious medallion and a poem clipped from a magazine. The poem read: "The clock of life is wound but once, and no man has the power to tell just when the hands will stop, at late or early hour. Now is the only time you own... Live, love, toil with a will. Place no faith in time. For the clocks may soon be still."

"How people treat you is their karma; how you react is yours."

Wayne Dyer

WHO AWHAT COMES AROUND **GOES AROUND**

Story 2:
World War II produced many heroes. One such man was Lieutenant Commander Butch O'Hare.

He was a fighter pilot assigned to the aircraft carrier Lexington in the South Pacific.

One day, his entire squadron was sent on a mission. After he was airborne, he looked at his fuel gauge and realised that someone had forgotten to top up his tank. He would not have enough fuel to complete his mission and get back to his ship.

His flight leader told him to return to the carrier. Reluctantly, he dropped out of formation and headed back to the fleet.

As he was returning, he saw something that turned his blood cold: a squadron of Japanese aircraft was speeding its way toward the American fleet.

The American fighters were gone on a sortie, and the fleet was all but defenceless. He couldn't reach his squadron and bring them back in time to save the fleet. Nor could he warn the fleet of the approaching danger. There was only one thing to do. He had to somehow divert them from the fleet.

Laying aside all thoughts of personal safety, he drove into the formation of Japanese planes. Wing-mounted 50 calibre guns blazed as he charged in, attacking one surprised enemy plane after another. Butch wove in and out of the now broken formation, firing at as many as possible until all his ammunition was finally spent.

Undaunted, he continued the assault. He drove at the planes, trying to clip a wing, or tail in hopes of damaging as many enemy planes as possible, rendering them unfit to fly.

Finally, the exasperated Japanese squadron took off in another direction.

"Make yourself indispensable and you'll be moved up. Act as if you're indispensable and you'll be moved out."

Anonymous

WHO AWHAT COMES AROUND **GOES AROUND**

> *Deeply relieved, Butch O'Hare and his tattered fighter limped back to the carrier.*
>
> *Upon arrival, he reported in and related the events surrounding his return. The film from the gun-camera mounted on his plane told the tale. It showed the extent of Butch's daring attempt to protect his fleet. He had, in fact, destroyed five enemy aircraft. This took place on 20 February 1942, and for that action Butch became the Navy's first Ace of WWII, and the first Naval Aviator to win the Medal of Honour.*
>
> *A year later Butch was killed in aerial combat at the age of 29. His home town would not allow the memory of this WWII hero to fade, and today O'Hare Airport in Chicago is named in tribute to the courage of this great man.*
>
> *So, the next time you find yourself at O'Hare International, give some thought to visiting Butch's memorial displaying his statue and his Medal of Honour. It's located between Terminals 1 and 2. So what do these two stories have to do with each other?*
>
> *Butch O'Hare was "Easy Eddie's" son.*

All great networkers have experienced the "What comes around goes around" life phenomenon. This is as a direct result of their abundance mentality: the two mindsets go hand-in-glove.

The "what comes around goes around" rule in networking encourages building a culture of support and generosity. For Introverts, this means finding ways to engage with people that aligns with their preferences and strengths, ensuring they can contribute to and benefit from their networks effectively.

"The energy you put out into the world always comes back to you."

Oprah Winfrey

WHO AWHAT COMES AROUND **GOES AROUND**

How can Introverts add the most value to their network?

Ideally you want to be the "go-to" person in your network.

Here are several strategies Introverts can use to add value and ensure mutual benefits within their professional and personal networks:

1. Leverage Deep Listening Skills
Introverts are excellent listeners - this is a skill that can be incredibly valuable in networking. By actively listening, Introverts can understand the needs, goals and challenges of their connections more deeply, allowing them to offer targeted, meaningful help or advice.

2. Provide Thoughtful Insights and Feedback
Due to their preference for deep thinking and reflection, Introverts can offer insightful feedback and solutions. When someone seeks advice or help, the thoughtful and considered perspectives of an Introvert can be highly valuable, fostering a strong appreciation and sense of reciprocity.

3. Engage in Written Communication
Introverts frequently excel in written communication, where they can articulate their thoughts and ideas more comfortably and effectively. Using emails, newsletters, blogs or social media platforms, Introverts can share knowledge, insights and resources with their network, adding value without the need for constant face-to-face interaction.

4. Build Deep, Meaningful Connections
Rather than trying to connect with everyone, Introverts can focus on building a few deep and meaningful relationships. These stronger connections are more likely to lead to meaningful exchanges of help,

Introvert Problems

What people think: vs **What the reality is:**

We are quiet, therefore we are:
- depressed
- mad
- sad
- bored
- indifferent
- shy
- arrogant

We are quiet, therefore we are:
- thinking
- listening
- daydreaming
- observing
- waiting for you finish speaking
- plotting
- recharing

@introvertmemes

advice and opportunities, creating a solid foundation for reciprocity.

5. Utilise One-on-One or Small Group Settings
Introverts thrive in one-on-one interactions or small group settings where conversations can be more meaningful and less overwhelming. Organising or participating in such settings enables Introverts to demonstrate their value and build rapport within their network without the drain of large social gatherings.

6. Showcase Expertise Through Content Creation
Creating content such as articles, podcasts or videos is an excellent way for Introverts to share their expertise and interests. This not only adds value to their network by providing useful information but also positions them as go-to experts in their field, encouraging others to seek them out for collaboration or advice.

7. Volunteer for Supportive Roles
Introverts can add value by volunteering for roles that support others, such as mentoring, committee work or organising events. These roles can leverage an Introvert's strengths in planning, listening and providing thoughtful feedback, while also building a culture of giving back within their network.

8. Focus on Quality Over Quantity
In all networking efforts, Introverts should focus on the quality of interactions rather than the quantity. Meaningful contributions, even if less frequent, are often more impactful and appreciated, fostering a strong sense of reciprocity and community.

By focusing on these strategies, Introverts can effectively add value to their networks in ways that are authentic and comfortable for them,

"You reap what you sow: Life is like a boomerang. Our thoughts, deeds, and words return to us sooner or later, with astounding accuracy."

Grant M. Bright

fostering an environment where reciprocity occurs naturally and both parties benefit.

If, however, you can't fulfil the needs of someone, you can refer to someone else in your network. By doing this you are still building your brand when you connect someone to a potential solution through your network.

Pay it Forward
Great networkers know that adding value is a key component of mutually beneficial business relationships.

You can add value by helping other people to get what they need when you:
- Connect prospective buyers and sellers.
- Make introductions to potential business partners or service providers.
- Gather information on a colleague's behalf.
- Share your expertise to help someone make a decision.
- Provide access to people, places and experiences.

If you can help solve a problem or create an opportunity someone wouldn't otherwise have, you've just generated tremendous tangible value within your network. Adding value is about being creative.

CHAPTER 12
THE ROLE OF **NETWORKS** IN **YOUR PROMOTION**

In their very useful Harvard Business Review article (2007) on "How leaders create and use Business Networks," Herminia Ibarra and Mark Lee Hunter recognises three forms of networking:

The Three Forms of Networking

Managers who think they are adept at networking are often operating only at an operational or personal level. Effective leaders learn to employ networks for strategic purposes.

	Operational	Personal	Strategic
Purpose	Getting work done efficiently; maintaining the capacities & functions required of the group.	Enhancing personal & professional development; providing referrals to useful information & contacts.	Figuring out future priorities & challenges; getting stakeholder support for them.
Location & temporal orientation	Contacts are mostly internal and orientated toward current demands.	Contacts are mostly external & orientated toward current interests & future potential interests.	Contacts are internal & external & orientated toward the future.
Players & recruitment	Key contacts are relatively non-discretionary; they are prescribed mostly by the task & organisational structure, so it is very clear who is relevant.	Key contacts are mostly discretionary; it is not always clear who is relevant.	Key contacts follow from the strategic context & the organisational environment, but specific membership is discretionary; it is not always clear who is relevant.
Network attributes & key behaviours	Depth: building strong working relationships.	Breadth: reaching out to contacts who can make referrals.	Leverage: creating inside-outside links.

*"**Networking isn't about making the most connections; it's about making the right connections.**"*

Michelle Tillis Lederman

THE ROLE OF **NETWORKS** IN **YOUR PROMOTION**

If Introverts are going to get promoted and achieve career fulfilment and success, they need to realise that effective leaders learn to employ networks for strategic purposes, moving beyond operational and personal networking.

Operational Networking

All good managers need to build good working relationships with the people who can help them do their jobs. The number and breadth of people involved can be impressive. These operational networks include not only direct reports and superiors, but also peers within an operational unit, other internal players with the power to block or support a project, and key outsiders such as suppliers, distributors and customers.

The purpose of this type of networking is to ensure coordination and cooperation among people who have to know and trust one another in order to accomplish their immediate tasks. That isn't always easy but it is relatively straightforward because the task provides focus and a clear criterion for membership in the network. Either you're necessary to the job and helping to get it done, or you're not.

Although operational networking was the form that came most naturally to the managers Ibarra and Hunter studied, nearly everyone had important blind spots regarding people and groups they depended on to make things happen.

In one case, Alistair, an accounting manager who worked in an entrepreneurial firm with several hundred employees, was suddenly promoted by the company's founder to financial director and given a seat on the board. He was the youngest and the least experienced

"Introverts excel at operational networking by focusing on creating strong, dependable relationships with colleagues and team members."

Nancy Ancowitz

THE ROLE OF **NETWORKS** IN **YOUR PROMOTION**

board member, but his instinctive response to these new responsibilities was to re-establish his functional credentials. Acting on a hint from the founder that the company might go public, Alistair undertook a re-organisation of the accounting department that would enable the books to withstand close scrutiny.

Alistair succeeded brilliantly in upgrading his team's capabilities but missed the fact that only a minority of the seven-person board shared the founder's ambition. A year into Alistair's tenure, discussion about whether to take the company public polarised the board. He discovered that all that time cleaning up the books might have been better spent sounding out his co-directors.

One of the problems with an exclusive reliance on operational networks is that they are usually geared toward meeting objectives as assigned, not toward asking the strategic question, "What *should* we be doing?"

Most operational networking occurs within an organisation and ties are determined by routine, short-term demands.

Relationships formed with outsiders, such as board members, customers and regulators, are directly task-related and tend to be bounded and constrained by demands determined at a higher level.

It's the quality of relationships — the rapport and mutual trust — that gives an operational network its power. Nonetheless, the substantial constraints on network membership mean these connections are unlikely to deliver value to managers beyond assistance with the task at hand.

"In operational networking, introverts can leverage their detail-oriented nature to ensure clear and effective communication with their peers."

Beth Buelow

THE ROLE OF **NETWORKS** IN **YOUR PROMOTION**

As a manager moves into a leadership role, their network must reorient itself externally and toward the future.

The typical manager in the group was more concerned with sustaining cooperation within the existing network than with building relationships to face non-routine or unforeseen challenges. But as a manager moves into a leadership role, their network must reorient itself externally and toward the future, whether they are an Introvert, Ambivert or Extrovert.

Personal Networking

Ibarra and Hunter observed that once aspiring leaders like Alistair awaken to the dangers of an excessively internal focus, they begin to seek kindred spirits outside their organisations.

Simultaneously, they become aware of the limitations of their social skills, such as a lack of knowledge about professional domains beyond their own, which makes it difficult for them to find common ground with people outside their usual circles.

Through professional associations, alumni groups, clubs and personal interest communities, managers gain new perspectives that allow them to advance in their careers. This is what the authors meant by personal networking.

Many of the managers they studied questioned why they should spend precious time on an activity so indirectly related to the work at hand. Why widen one's circle of casual acquaintances when there isn't time even for urgent tasks? The answer is that these contacts provide important referrals, information, and often developmental support such as coaching and mentoring.

"Personal networking is about forming deep, meaningful connections. Introverts shine in these one-on-one interactions."

Sophia Dembling

THE ROLE OF **NETWORKS** IN **YOUR PROMOTION**

A newly-appointed factory director, when faced with a turnaround- or- close-down situation that was paralysing his staff, joined a business organisation — and met a lawyer who became his counsel in the turnaround. Buoyed by his success, he networked within his company's headquarters in search of someone who had dealt with a similar crisis. Eventually, he found two mentors to help him with the turn-around.

A personal network can also be a safe space for personal development and can provide a foundation for strategic networking. I joined EO (Entrepreneurs Organisation) five years ago. EO is a global association of founder CEOs with a minimum business turnover of $1 million. I've found invaluable insights from fellow entrepreneurs on growing my business through this network. Entrepreneurship can be lonely, but I found my personal networking tribe.

Personal networks are largely external, made up of discretionary links to people with something in common. As a result, what makes a personal network powerful is its referral potential. According to the famous six degrees of separation principle, our personal contacts are valuable to the extent that they help us reach, with as few connections as possible, the far-off person who has the information we need.

In watching managers struggle to widen their professional relationships in ways that feel both natural and legitimate to them, Ibarra and Hunter repeatedly saw them shift their time and energy from operational to personal networking.

For people who have rarely looked outside their organisations, this is an important first step, one that fosters a deeper understanding of themselves and the environments in which they move. Ultimately, however, personal networking alone won't propel managers through the leadership transition.

> "*Introverts can thrive in personal networking by investing time in a few close relationships rather than spreading themselves too thin.*"

Susan Cain

THE ROLE OF **NETWORKS** IN **YOUR PROMOTION**

Aspiring leaders may find people who awaken new interests but fail to become comfortable with the power players at the level above them. Or they may achieve new influence within a professional community but fail to harness those ties in the service of organisational goals.

That's why managers who know they may still need to develop their networking skills, and make a real effort to do so, feel like they have wasted their time and energy. As we'll see, personal networking will not help a manager through the leadership transition unless they learn how to bring those connections to bear on organisational strategy.

Strategic Networking

When managers begin the delicate transition from functional manager to business leader, they must start to concern themselves with broad strategic issues. Lateral and vertical relationships with other functional and business unit managers — all people outside their immediate control — become a lifeline for figuring out how their own contributions fit into the big picture. Strategic networking plugs the aspiring leader into a set of relationships and information sources that collectively embody the power to achieve personal and organisational goals.

Operating beside players with diverse affiliations, backgrounds, objectives and incentives requires a manager to formulate business, rather than functional objectives, and to work through the coalitions and networks needed to sell ideas and compete for resources.

Consider Sophie, a manager who, after rising steadily through the ranks in logistics and distribution, was stupefied to learn that the CEO was considering a radical re-organisation of her function that would strip her of some responsibilities.

"Introverts can excel at strategic networking by carefully selecting events and opportunities that align with their career goals and personal values."

Marti Olsen Laney

THE ROLE OF NETWORKS IN YOUR PROMOTION

Rewarded to date for incremental annual improvements, she had failed to notice shifting priorities in the wider market and the resulting internal shuffle for resources and power at the higher levels of her company.

Although she had built a loyal, high-performing team, she had few relationships outside her group to help her anticipate the new imperatives, let alone give her ideas about how to respond. After she argued that distribution issues were her purview but failed to be persuasive, she hired consultants to help her prepare a counter-proposal. But Sophie's boss simply concluded that she lacked a broad, longer-term business perspective. Frustrated, Sophie contemplated leaving the company. Only after some patient coaching from a senior manager did she understand that she had to get out of her unit and start talking to opinion leaders inside and outside the company to form a sellable plan for the future.

What differentiates a leader from a manager, research tells us, is the ability to figure out where to go and to enlist the people and groups necessary to get there. Recruiting stakeholders, lining up allies and sympathisers, diagnosing the political landscape and brokering conversations among unconnected parties are all part of a leader's job. As they step up to the leadership transition, some managers accept their growing dependence on others and seek to transform it into mutual influence. Others dismiss such work as "political" and, as a result, undermine their ability to advance their goals.

The key to a good strategic network is leverage: the ability to marshal information, support and resources from one sector of a network to achieve results in another. Strategic networkers use indirect influence, convincing one person in the network to get someone else, who is not in the network, to take a needed action.

NETWORKING FOR **INTROVERTS**

"In strategic networking, introverts can use their strengths in research and preparation to make informed and impactful connections."

Michaela Chung

THE ROLE OF **NETWORKS** IN **YOUR PROMOTION**

Strategic networkers don't just influence their relational environment. They shape it in their own image by moving and hiring subordinates, changing suppliers and sources of financing, lobbying to place allies in peer positions, and even restructuring their boards to create networks favourable to their business goals.

Strategic networking can be difficult for emerging leaders because it absorbs a significant amount of the time and energy that managers usually devote to meeting their many operational demands. This is one reason why many managers drop their strategic networking precisely when they need it most: when their units are in trouble and only outside support can rescue them. The trick is not to hide in the operational network but to develop it into a more strategic one.

One manager in the author's study, used lateral and functional contacts throughout his firm to resolve tensions with his boss that resulted from substantial differences in style and strategic approaches between the two. Tied down in operational chores at a distant location, the manager had lost contact with headquarters. He resolved the situation by simultaneously obliging his direct reports to take on more of the local management effort and sending messages through his network that would help bring him back into the loop with the boss.

Operational, personal and strategic networks are not mutually exclusive. One manager we studied used his personal passion, hunting, to meet people from professions as diverse as stonemasonry and household moving. Almost none of these hunting friends had anything to do with his work in the consumer electronics industry, yet they all had to deal with one of his own daily concerns: customer relations. Hearing about their problems and techniques allowed him to view his own from a different perspective and helped him define principles that he could test in his work.

NETWORKING FOR **INTROVERTS**

"Introverts can thrive in strategic networking by identifying and targeting key individuals who align with their career aspirations and values."

William Arruda

THE ROLE OF NETWORKS IN YOUR PROMOTION

Ultimately, what began as a personal network of hunting partners became operationally and strategically valuable to this manager. The key was his ability to build outside-in links for maximum leverage. But we've seen others who avoided networking, or failed at it, because they let interpersonal chemistry, not strategic needs, determine which relationships they cultivated.

Work from the outside in

One of the most daunting aspects of strategic networking is that there often seems to be no natural "excuse" for making contact with a more senior person outside one's function or business unit. It's difficult to build a relationship with anyone, let alone a senior executive, without a reason for interacting, like a common task or a shared purpose.

Some successful managers find common ground from the outside-in by transposing a personal interest into the strategic domain. Linda Henderson is a good example. An investment banker responsible for a group of media industry clients, she always wondered how to connect to some of her senior colleagues who served other industries. She resolved to make time for an extracurricular passion, the theatre, in a way that would enhance her business development activities. Four times a year, her secretary booked a dinner at a downtown hotel and reserved a block of theatre tickets. Key clients were invited. Through these events, Linda not only developed her own business but also learned about her clients' companies in a way that generated ideas for other parts of her firm, thus enabling her to engage with colleagues.

"In strategic networking, introverts can use their strengths in research and preparation to build valuable, purposeful connections."

Adam Grant

THE ROLE OF **NETWORKS** IN **YOUR PROMOTION**

Other managers build outside-in connections by using their functional interests or expertise. For example, communities of practice exist (or can easily be created on the Internet) in almost every area of business, from brand management, to Six Sigma, to global strategy.

Savvy managers reach out to kindred spirits outside their organisations to contribute and multiply their knowledge. The information they glean, in more cases than not, becomes the "hook" for making internal connections.

Re-allocate your time

If an aspiring leader has not yet mastered the art of delegation, he or she will find many reasons not to spend time networking. Participating in formal and informal meetings with people in other units takes time away from functional responsibilities and internal team affairs. Between the obvious pay-off of a task accomplished and the ambiguous, often delayed rewards of networking, naive managers repeatedly choose the former. The less they practice networking, the less efficient at it they become, creating a vicious cycle.

Effective business leaders spend a lot of time every day gathering the information they need to meet their goals, relying on informal discussions with a lot of people who are not necessarily in charge of an issue or task. They network to obtain information continually, not just at formal meetings.

> *"Strategic networking is about connecting with people who can help you achieve your long-term goals. Introverts can excel by being intentional and thoughtful in their networking efforts."*
>
> Dorie Clark

THE ROLE OF **NETWORKS** IN **YOUR PROMOTION**

Ask and you shall receive

Many managers equate having a good network with having a large databaseof contacts or attending high-profile professional conferences and events. People kick off a networking initiative by improving their record-keeping or adopting a network management tool. But they falter at the next step — picking up the phone. Instead, they wait until they need something *badly*. The best networkers do exactly the opposite: they take every opportunity to give to, and receive from, the network, not only when they need to.

A network lives and thrives only when it is used. A good way to begin is to make a simple request or take the initiative to connect two people who would benefit from meeting each other. Doing something — anything — gets the ball rolling and builds confidence that one does, in fact, have something to contribute.

For Introverts this is one of the hardest steps. My advice is, "Don't overthink – just ask!" It will get easier with practice.

Stick to it

It takes a while to reap the benefits of networking. We have seen many managers resolve to put networking at the top of their agendas, only to be derailed by the first crisis that comes along.

One example is Harris Roberts, a regulatory affairs expert who realised he needed a broader network to achieve his goal of becoming a business unit manager. To force himself into what felt like an "unnatural act," Harris volunteered to be the liaison for his business school cohort's alumni network. But six months later, when a major new drug approval

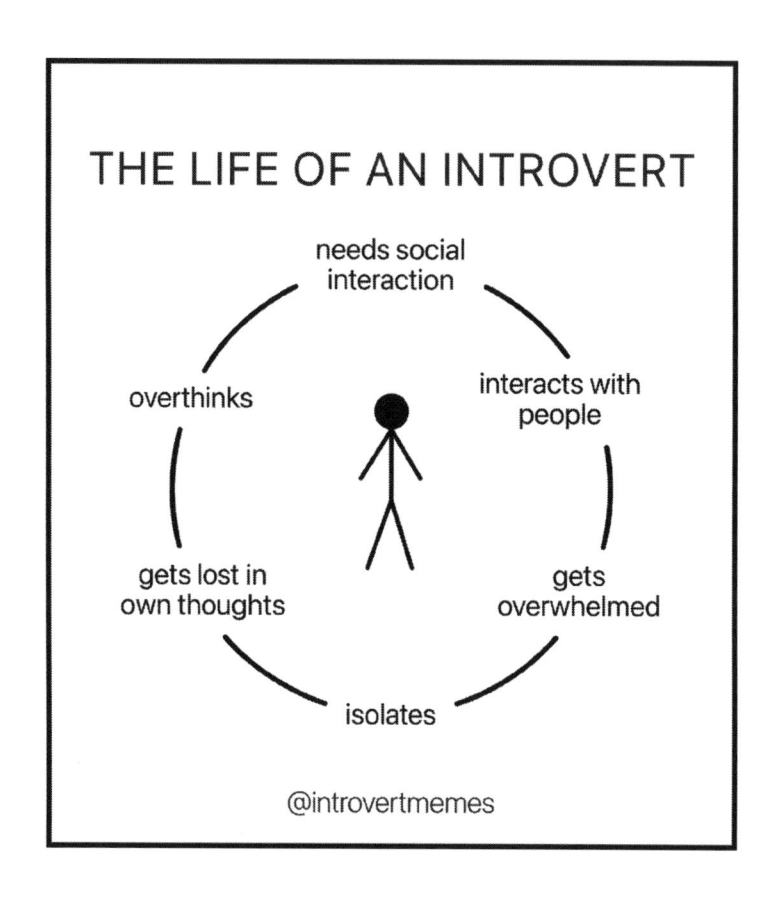

NETWORKING FOR **INTROVERTS**

THE LIFE OF AN INTROVERT

- needs social interaction
- interacts with people
- gets overwhelmed
- isolates
- gets lost in own thoughts
- overthinks

@introvertmemes

THE ROLE OF **NETWORKS** IN **YOUR PROMOTION**

process overwhelmed his calendar, Harris dropped all outside activities. Two years later, he found himself out of touch and still a functional manager. He failed to recognise that by not taking the time to attend industry conferences or compare notes with his peers, he was missing out on the strategic perspective and information that would make him a more attractive candidate for promotion.

Building a leadership network is less a matter of skill than of will. When first efforts do not bring quick rewards, some may simply conclude that networking isn't among their talents. But networking is not a talent, nor does it require a gregarious, extroverted personality. It is a skill, one that takes practice. Ibarra and Hunter have seen over and over again that people who work at networking can learn not only how to do it well but also how to enjoy it. They also tend to be more successful than those who fail to leverage external ties, or insist on defining their jobs narrowly.

NETWORKING FOR **INTROVERTS**

CHAPTER 13
WHERE THE RUBBER HITS THE ROAD
- NETWORKING FUNCTIONS

As an Introvert, navigating cocktail functions and similar social gatherings can be challenging but it is entirely manageable with the right strategies in place.

Zoya Mabuto-Mokoditoa, CEO and Founder of Zoya Speaks and one of our A-Team tribe members and facilitators on our programmes, quotes the *Black Panther* movie where the grandmother tells the young grandson, "Show them who you are."

Being at functions is an opportunity to show people who you are. To be present to others you must invest the time and energy to be present to who you are. One of the exercises she gets delegates to do before they arrive at an event is to think of three things about themselves that make them who they are, and then think about how they can reveal that.

If kindness is one of your defining characteristics, then think about how you can reveal that about yourself. It could be in a story you share, or how you could potentially assist someone at the event to solve a problem. Zoya also shares a wonderful "Empty Space" exercise that is very well

NETWORKING FOR **INTROVERTS**

"Maybe I'll come" — "I'm not coming"

"I'll let you know" — "I'm not coming"

"I'm not sure yet" — "I'm very sure that I'm not coming"

"I'll try and come" — "I won't try anything"

"I'll think about it" — "I won't think about anything, I'm not coming"

@introvertmemes

received by Introverts. She asks them to look at the empty space they are about to enter and focus on the unique value they are going to fill that space with.

The feedback from delegates has been that they're no longer grounded in what other people think – they are instead focusing on their unique value. One Introvert delegate said the activity made her feel like "she was tall on the outside." Confidence then no longer becomes outer work. It is the inner work of being grounded in yourself and your value, which other people get then to experience outwardly in you.

Here are some other practical tips that can help make these events more enjoyable and productive:

1. Prepare Mentally
Spend time preparing mentally for the event. This could involve reviewing the guest list if available, setting specific goals for the event (like whom you want to meet), or simply reminding yourself of the purpose of attending. Mental preparation can help reduce anxiety and increase your confidence.

Debbie Goodman, founder and CEO of Jackhammer Executive Search, a self-confessed and highly successful Introvert, says she sets herself a goal to meet two new people at an event. She prepares herself mentally for this and only allows herself to leave when she's done that.

2. Arrive Early
Arriving early can be advantageous because it's easier to start conversations when the environment is less crowded and noisy. It also gives you the chance to get comfortable with the space before it

NETWORKING FOR **INTROVERTS**

> Feels like the life of an introvert boils down to working up the energy to act like an extrovert, until you can go home and be comfortably introverted.
>
> @introvertmemes

fills up, and you might even strike up a conversation with other early arrivals who could be more inclined to introduce you to others later on.

3. Have a Plan
Think about some conversation starters or questions you can ask to initiate conversations. People love talking about themselves, so asking open-ended questions about their work, interests, or how they're connected to the event can be a good strategy. Having a few topics in mind can ease the stress of initiating conversations.

4. Seek Out Other Introverts
Look for others who might also be feeling a bit out of place or who are standing alone. They're likely to be grateful for the interaction and you might find it easier to talk to someone who understands how you're feeling.

5. Take Breaks
Recognise when you're feeling drained and take short breaks to recharge. This could mean stepping outside for a breath of fresh air or finding a quiet corner for a few minutes. Listen to your energy levels and give yourself permission to take a moment when needed.

6. Set Realistic Expectations
Instead of pressuring yourself to meet everyone, focus on making a few meaningful connections. Quality often trumps quantity, especially when it comes to networking and building relationships.

7. Use Listening to Your Advantage
Introverts are great listeners. Use this skill to your advantage by really engaging with the people you talk to. Showing genuine interest can make your conversations more memorable and meaningful.

"Networking isn't about being the loudest voice in the room; it's about being the most genuine. Introverts excel in authenticity."

Adam Grant

8. Follow Up
After the event, follow up with the people you met. Sending a brief email or LinkedIn message mentioning something specific from your conversation can be a great way to reinforce the connection. This step is crucial and can sometimes be more important than the initial meeting.

Cocktail functions and similar events can feel less daunting over time as you find strategies that work for you. Embrace your Introvert nature and remember that your approach to networking can be just as effective, albeit different, from more Extrovert strategies.

HOW TO BREAK INTO CONVERSATIONS

Joni Peddie, CEO of Resilient People and behaviourist says that Introverts need to MAXIMISE the first minute, before their anxiety takes over.

"The Minute to Win it" approach works
- Make an effort to engage within the first 30 seconds to a minute of the conversation. This gets you over the hurdle, and gets you going. It's a pro-active approach that helps set a positive tone for the conversation.

The "rule of three" is a helpful guideline for Introverts looking to break into conversations. It suggests that you look for groups of three people to join. It's more likely that at least one person is not actively engaged in the conversation at any given moment, making it easier for you to enter the discussion without interrupting. Groups of four are too big and

Breaking Into Conversation Technique

you'll find you're interrupting a two-way conversation with groups of two. This is a very important technique. If you don't use it, you will end up recycling your existing network and not meeting new people.

Here's how to apply this rule effectively:

1. Observe and Choose Wisely
Scan the room for groups of three, observing their body language and facial expressions. Go and stand next to them, and unobtrusively listen and overhear their conversation.

This is the most important step, because if you have nothing in common with their conversation or feel you have nothing of value to add then you can move on swiftly, without even breaking into the conversation in the first place.

I was at an Investment Banking cocktail party recently where there were many Investment bankers and people from financial services. I stood next to the first group of three people, considering if I should break into their conversation, only to find they were talking about derivatives. I know nothing and have no curiosity about derivatives, so I quickly realised it was a waste of energy breaking in.

It's crucial for Introverts to manage their energy at big events. Taking the time to consider which groups of people you have something in common with, or can add value to, is a critical step in event networking for Introverts.

"You are only one conversation away from completely changing your life."

Helen Nicholson

2. Join in with a Smile
Once you've identified a group, approach them confidently but casually, with a smile. Your non-verbal cues can communicate your friendly intentions even before you speak.

3. Use an Open-Ended Question to Join In
When you find a suitable moment, introduce yourself and ask an open-ended question related to the current topic or something that can naturally steer the conversation in a new direction. For example, "That's an interesting point. How do you think that will impact the industry in the next few years?"

4. Mention How You Relate to the Topic
Sharing something about yourself in relation to the topic can help make the connection more personal and engaging. For instance, "I've actually been reading a lot about that issue; it seems like it's going to be a major challenge for us."

5. Engage Everyone in the Group
Try to engage everyone in the group, not just the person you first speak to. Making eye contact with all members and directing questions or comments to different individuals can help you become part of the group more seamlessly.

6. Give Yourself Permission to Exit
If the conversation doesn't seem to be a good fit, or if you've contributed and would like to meet more people, it's okay to exit the conversation gracefully. You can say something like, "It was great chatting with you. I'm going to mingle a bit more but I hope to catch up with you later on."

NETWORKING FOR **INTROVERTS**

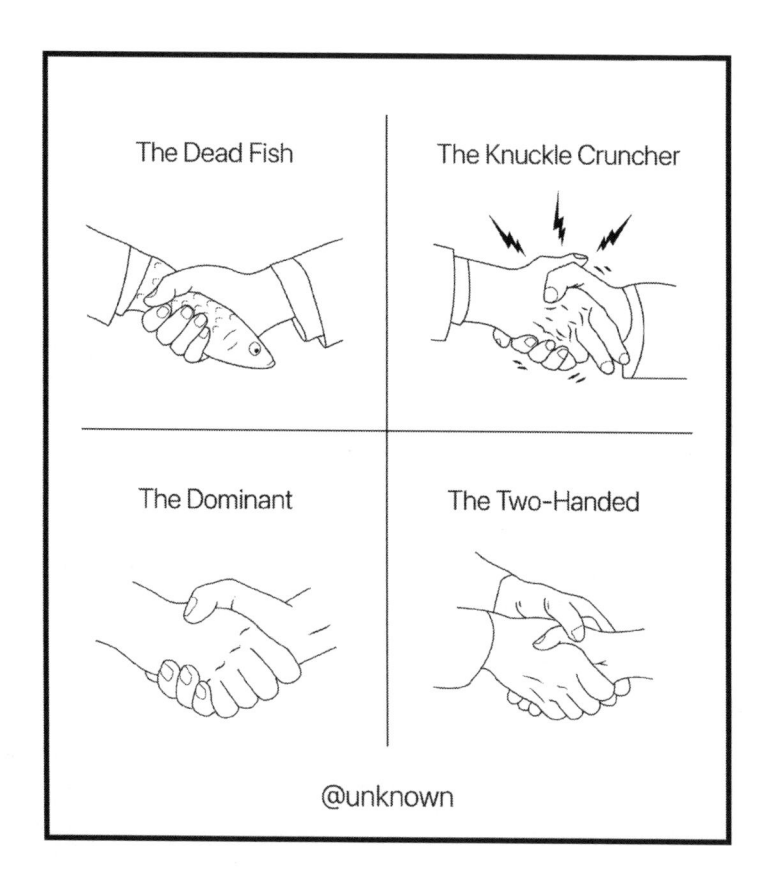

The Dead Fish	The Knuckle Cruncher
The Dominant	The Two-Handed

@unknown

Using the "rule of three" can help Introverts find a comfortable way to break into conversations at events. By choosing the right moment and engaging in a friendly, inclusive manner, you can turn networking opportunities into enjoyable and fruitful interactions.

THE INFLUENTIAL HANDSHAKE

Make sure you have the right handshake. Influential people make an immediate connection with everyone they meet. Handshakes are an important first touch point when greeting people. Which handshake do you have?

- **The Dead Fish:** When one hand is extended into another but there is barely any movement of the hand/wrist.

- **The Knuckle Cruncher:** Too much force – the violator is either someone who doesn't know their own strength, or they are someone who is trying to prove that they should be taken seriously.

- **The Dominant:** This happens when the hand's palm is extended down, which symbolizes the offender having the "upper hand". The opposite of this is "The Twisting Dominant", which is where the hand is normal at first, but then twists to gain the upper hand once contact is made.

- **The Two-Handed, or Politician's Handshake:** This happens when the other person uses their free hand to cover the handshake or the other person's wrist, arm and shoulder.

Most influential people use an authentic Two-Handed Handshake, enveloping the other person's hand between theirs to demonstrate how pleased they are to meet the other person. This handshake must come from a place of authenticity and not look as if you've been on a networking 101 training programme.

NETWORKING FOR **INTROVERTS**

CHAPTER 14
BEST SMALL TALK TECHNIQUE
OBSERVE, ASK AND REVEAL

Small talk leads to big talk, so it is important and something you need to get better at, if you're going to meet new people at an event.

Every time you walk into a school function for your children, a cocktail function or a conference, I'd like you to think of rowing as you walk in. The OAR (Observe, Ask and Reveal) technique coined first by the Networking Expert, Susan Roane, is one I've found very useful to get conversations going.

It involves making an **Observation,**

Asking a question based on that observation,

and then **Revealing something** about yourself in relation to the topic.

The reveal is the secret sauce of this technique – when you reveal something vulnerable about yourself first, you're showing you're not a "know-it-all" and that you're humbly engaging in conversation.

NETWORKING FOR **INTROVERTS**

How small talk feels to an introvert

@introvertmemes

Sometimes you need to use a few Observe, Ask and Reveals to get the conversation started but it works every time.

Here are some examples:

At a Professional Networking Event – (this actually happened to me)

Observe: You're at an investor event and you notice you're the only female.
Ask: "I seem to be the only woman interested in investing; how long have you been investing for?"
Reveal: "I'm a novice investor and this is the first time I've been to an event like this. I'd welcome any advice."

At a Casual Social Gathering

Observe: Someone is wearing a T-shirt with a logo of a famous rock band.
Ask: "Is that a T-shirt for The Rolling Stones? Do you listen to their music?"
Reveal: "I love their music! 'Paint It Black' has to be one of my all-time favorites. I've always found their energy contagious, even just from their recordings."

At a Work-related Cocktail Party

Observe: You notice someone's unique cocktail drink.
Ask: "That's an interesting drink you've chosen. What is it?"
Reveal: "I usually stick to wine but I've been wanting to try something new. Maybe I'll give that a try next. I love exploring interesting cocktails."

"Small talk is the seed that can grow into a meaningful conversation and a lasting connection."

Debra Fine

BEST SMALL TALK TECHNIQUE

At a Neighborhood Barbecue/Braai

Observe: Someone's pet dog is playing nearby.
Ask: "Your dog seems to have a lot of energy. What breed is he?"
Reveal: "I've always admired that breed's intelligence and loyalty. I grew up with a dog that was a big part of our family, and I'm considering adopting one myself."

Using the "Observe, Ask, Reveal" technique, Introverts can navigate small talk by steering conversations towards subjects of mutual interest, making interactions more engaging and less stressful. This approach also allows for the exchange of information and experiences, making conversations more meaningful and memorable.

SMALL TALK NO-NO'S

1. Being unprepared – not having your elevator pitch ready (more on that in Chapter Sixteen).
2. Not being well-informed by reading news and being abreast of influential business news.
3. Killing conversations by:
   - Asking a barrage of questions, no matter how open-ended, and not listening to the answers. Introverts are unlikely to do this – you can see why networking events can actually be your SUPERPOWER.
   - Complaining – it sets a bad tone for your Personal Brand.
   - One-upping and competing – it closes the door on conversations. No-one wants to chat to someone who is arrogant and egotistical. Again, Introverts are unlikely to do this!
   - Using bad language.

BEST SMALL TALK TECHNIQUE

- Interrupting while someone is talking. It sends out the message that someone is less important or interesting than others in the room.
- Scanning the room with your eyes while you're speaking to another person. It sends out the message that the person you're chatting to is less important than everyone else.

NETWORKING FOR **INTROVERTS**

CHAPTER 15
EVENT ETIQUETTE
– GET THE MOST OUT OF EVENTS

Name Tags and Name-Remembering Techniques

Always, always wear your name tag at an event on the right-hand side. Although men's shirt pockets are on the left-hand side and it's easier to clip the name tag there, it's better to clip it on the right-hand side. It will be in the other person's line of sight as you both extend your right arm for a handshake.

I'm not a fan of lanyard name tags as they turn around, and almost always hang around people's stomachs, which is not where you want anyone's focus to be!

Remembering people's names is not a natural strength for most of us. It comes up in our workshops as a big stumbling block when meeting new people. A great technique is to say someone's name three times in conversation. Firstly, when they've introduced themselves repeat their name, and if it's a tricky name or you don't hear what the person has said, then repeat it and ask them if you've pronounced it properly.

NETWORKING FOR **INTROVERTS**

Remembering Names Technique

"My name is Helen, Helen, Helen"

EVENT ETIQUETTE – GET THE MOST OUT OF EVENTS

Secondly, repeat their name during the conversation, and thirdly when you exit the conversation say, "xxxx, it was wonderful to meet you and I look forward to staying connected."

What do we do if we forget a name:
- Tell the truth. Don't waste your time trying to remember how you were supposed to remember the person's name. Instead, simply say, "It's been one of those days. I remember you but please help me out with your name." Say it lightly and apologetically. People understand. It's happened to them!
- Stick your hand out and say your name. People respond saying their name 95% of the time. Believe me, if you've forgotten their name, they've probably forgotten yours too.
- If you're with other people, introduce your companion and hopefully the other person introduces themself. If you're alone, unfortunately you must "fess up!" It's not a big deal – look comfortable and everyone understands forgetting people's names.

How To Exit A Conversation Elegantly

Exiting a conversation gracefully at an event is an important skill, helping to ensure that both you and the people you're speaking with feel respected and positive about the interaction. Here are some tactful ways to leave a conversation:

"It's the people we hardly know, and not our closest friends, who will improve our lives most dramatically."

Meg Jay

EVENT ETIQUETTE – GET THE MOST OUT OF EVENTS

1. Express Appreciation
Begin by expressing your gratitude for the conversation. Something simple like, "It was really great talking to you, about [topic]" can affirm the value of the interaction and leave a positive impression.

2. Use a Polite Close
Offer a polite and straightforward close that signals the conversation is ending. For example, "I've enjoyed our chat so much. Thank you - was so good meeting you."

3. Offer to Connect Later
If you're interested in continuing the conversation at another time, suggest exchanging contact information or connecting on social media. Saying something like, "I'd love to continue this conversation. Can we exchange emails?" is a good way to keep the door open for future interactions.

4. Make an Introduction
If appropriate, introduce the person to someone else nearby before excusing yourself. This can help transition the conversation and ensure they're not left standing alone. "Before I go, let me introduce you to [Name], who has interesting insights on [topic]."

5. End on a Positive Note
Regardless of how the conversation went, aim to end on a positive note. A simple, "Enjoy the rest of your evening!" can be a friendly and positive way to conclude the interaction.

6. Excuse Yourself Politely
Sometimes a simple and direct approach works best. Saying, "Excuse me, I need to step away for a moment," is perfectly acceptable. Just be sure to say it with a smile and in a polite tone.

NETWORKING FOR **INTROVERTS**

"Networking is not just about collecting contacts. It's about planting relationships."

MiShaat

EVENT **ETIQUETTE** – GET THE **MOST OUT OF EVENTS**

I also start to walk over to the food station or bar if I'm speaking to one person and want to exit the conversation. We mirror each other's body language and generally you'll find the other person will walk alongside you. It's easier to find someone to introduce the other person to at the food/bar station, while you make a graceful exit.

NETWORKING FOR **INTROVERTS**

CHAPTER 16
YOUR ELEVATOR **PITCH**

An elevator pitch is a 20-second sound bite describing what you do – in simple language that an eight-year-old child can understand – in the time that it takes to ride up an elevator.

It's not a sales pitch. It's a brief introduction of who you are and what you can do, so that you can start a business conversation. It provides a "hook" into what you do.

The key element of a good elevator pitch is that it focuses on what problem you solve, and not your job title.

When we focus on our job title it doesn't give any reason for the person you are meeting to continue a conversation, as there's nothing in it for them.

In our networking workshops I always show a picture of my 27-year-old twins Sabrina and Caitlyn when they were little, as an example of the natural self-orientation we generally have when we meet new people. Sabrina and Caitlyn are my dream – they're not anyone else's dream. I need to move away from that self-orientation to, "What's in it for them?" A good elevator pitch enables me to do that.

NETWORKING FOR **INTROVERTS**

My twin daughters, Sabrina and Caitlyn

YOUR ELEVATOR PITCH

The best formula I've encountered is:

I'm....
I specialise/do this.....
So that........

What makes a successful elevator pitch?
1. It's quick and punchy.
2. It comes across naturally (even though you need to rehearse it).
3. It opens up the conversation.
4. It's interesting enough to make your listener want to find out more.
5. It briefly describes what you do and how this benefits the other person.

Everyone you meet cares about what you can do for them.

Are you an Investment Banker? No – you specialise in financing deals, so that a country's economy can prosper and grow.

Are you an auditor? No – you are the CSI of accountants who specialises in keeping companies finances in order, so that shareholders can sleep well at night.

Are you in IT? No – you save companies money and time using technology.

I had two examples of failing at delivering a good elevator pitch at the beginning of my career and I realised how I had missed out on potential opportunities.

Formula for a great elevator speech

- I'm ...
- I do this ...
- So that...

YOUR ELEVATOR PITCH

The first involved Oprah Winfrey. I live in Johannesburg, South Africa. Oprah often visits our city when she visits the school she built here, to advance the lives of talented, under-privileged girls. She has a specific hotel she likes to stay in, and I was at the same hotel attending a girlfriend's birthday breakfast.

I went to the buffet counter, and there standing in front of me was Oprah and her best friend Gayle. They were both in their sweatpants and sweating profusely after an exercise workout. I ignored Oprah completely and carried on dishing up my breakfast, mainly because I didn't know how to start a conversation at that stage in my career and had no idea what to say to Oprah. I hadn't learned
 - How to do small talk
 - How to deliver a great elevator pitch

I always regret that moment. I'm unlikely to ever bump into Oprah again – I regret telling her how much I admire the work she does in South Africa. It was a missed opportunity and I should have seized the moment. Introverts have confessed that's how they feel often – they just don't know how to start a conversation.

As a result of reading this book you are not in that boat anymore. You've learned all the power "small-talk", breaking-into-conversation skills so that you'll never be left on the networking back foot again.

The second example of bad networking happened when I was standing in a buffet queue for lunch at a conference. A CEO was ahead of me and while he was dishing out his meal, he asked me what I did. I replied that I was in training. I could see his eyes glaze over, as he lost interest in what I had to say. I don't blame him – I was bored myself. I had given him no reason to continue our conversation or a, "What's in it for him?" hook to initiate a conversation.

"For introverts, an elevator speech serves as a lifeline, turning potential awkward encounters into opportunities to shine."

Unknown

YOUR ELEVATOR **PITCH**

In hindsight, after learning the powerful elevator pitch formula, I should have said, "My name is Helen Nicholson. I founded The Networking Company, a leadership training company. We specialise in training people in corporates on the soft power skills like personal branding and networking so that people can grow, be retained and be promoted."

The two key issues a CEO is concerned with:
   - Retention and growth of key staff

I have addressed both these needs in the new improved version of my elevator pitch.

I never had a second opportunity to meet that CEO. You don't always get a second chance to make a first impression. That's why I advise people to practise their elevator pitch when they are sitting in the traffic. You do need to rehearse it so that it sounds natural, because often when you're put on the spot you freeze. I had that feedback often from the Introverts I interviewed – they often thought of great introductions when the event was over.

Ideally you need three versions of the "so that...." in your elevator pitches for three different target markets:
   - Family/friends
   - Colleagues (where you can use acronyms or jargon you are all familiar with).
   - Potential clients

> Introverts when the elevator doors close before anyone can get on
>
> @introvertmemes

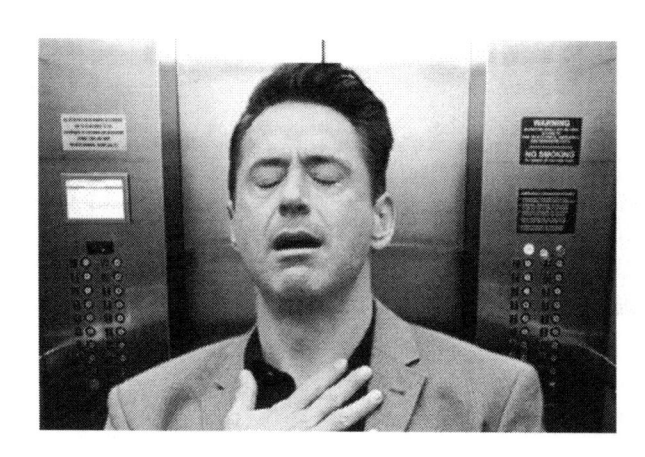

So different versions of mine would be:

FAMILY/SOCIAL
"My name is Helen. I founded The Networking Company 20 years ago, a leadership training company. We specialise in training people in corporates on the soft power skills like personal branding and networking so that people can grow and develop."

COLLEAGUE
"My name is Helen Nicholson. I founded The Networking Company 20 years ago, a leadership training company. We specialise in training people in corporates on the soft power skills like personal branding and networking so that people can be promoted.

CLIENT/ENTREPRENEUR
"My name is Helen Nicholson. I founded The Networking Company 20 years ago, a leadership training company. We specialise in training people on the soft power skills like personal branding and networking so that entrepreneurs can grow their businesses.

The best elevator pitch I've ever heard is:
"I'm the underwire bra of the organisation." It was from a data- capturer who believed their role supported everyone else in the organisation.

Another great elevator pitch was from a janitor who worked at NASA (National Aeronautic and Space Administration) in America. When asked what he did for a living, he replied:

"I put people on the moon."

"You never get a second chance to make a first impression."

Unknown

YOUR ELEVATOR PITCH

He wasn't wrong. By cleaning the bathrooms, he ensured the hygiene and well-being of everyone who worked on the space station, including the astronauts. And it certainly captures your attention!

Elevator pitches can be particularly challenging for Introverts, who might find the prospect of pitching themselves or their ideas in a brief, high-pressure situation daunting. Go back to Zoya's advice in Chapter Thirteen where she spoke about remembering three of your unique characteristics before you enter a new room. That clarity and confidence will influence you in delivering a powerful Elevator Pitch.

Here are some tips tailored for Introverts:

Practise, Practise, Practise: Rehearse your pitch in a comfortable environment until you feel confident. Practice with friends, family or in front of a mirror. The more familiar

Take Deep Breaths: Before you start, take a moment to breathe deeply. This can help calm your nerves and improve your delivery.

Embrace Pauses: Don't be afraid to pause for a moment if you need to collect your thoughts. Pauses can be powerful and give your listener a moment to absorb what you've said.

Remember, the key for Introverts to deliver better elevator pitches lies in leveraging their strengths, preparing thoroughly and practicing regularly to build confidence and ease in delivery.

NETWORKING FOR **INTROVERTS**

CHAPTER 17
THE ART OF THE FOLLOW-UP
(AN INTROVERT SUPERPOWER)

Following up is a critical skill in networking, acting as the bridge between initial contact and developing a meaningful, productive relationship over time. Introverts are typically much better at following up after meeting a new person than Extroverts, so really zone in on this superpower.

Research indicates you should follow-up within three days of meeting someone new. The networking window of opportunity stays open for three days. After that, it's trickier for people to remember you. Ideally you want to honour your promise of connecting, as it demonstrates that you're a person of your word, reliable and trustworthy.

Here are some of the other key reasons why follow-up is so important:

Strengthens Connections
Following up after an initial meeting or conversation shows that you value the connection and are interested in keeping the dialogue going. It's a fundamental step in turning a brief encounter into a lasting relationship.

"Introverts may not thrive in initial interactions, but they excel in follow-ups, where they can connect on a deeper, more genuine level."

Unknown

Keeps You Memorable
People meet numerous individuals at networking events, in meetings, and through their daily professional activities. A timely follow-up can set you apart from others, keeping you top of mind with your new connections.

Creates Opportunities for Collaboration
Following up can lead to opportunities for collaboration that were discussed in initial conversations. It can open doors to projects, partnerships, job offers or other forms of collaboration that might not have materialised without that nudge.

Facilitates the Exchange of Value
Networking is fundamentally about the mutual exchange of value. Following up allows you to explore how you and your new contact can help each other, whether through sharing information, resources or opportunities.

Allows You to Clarify and Elaborate
Initial conversations can be brief due to time constraints. Following up gives you a chance to clarify any points that were rushed and provide additional information that can make your interaction more meaningful.

Helps Build Trust
By following up and keeping in touch, you build trust with your contacts. This trust is the foundation of any strong professional relationship.

"The follow-up is an introvert's secret weapon; it's the perfect opportunity to shine through thoughtful, deliberate communication."

Unknown

THE ART OF THE **FOLLOW-UP**

Social media also plays an important role in following up and that's why it's so important for you to regularly post and update your social media, especially LinkedIn, as it's a great way to stay top of mind with your network.

Effective follow-up involves more than just a single email or call after meeting someone. It's about fostering a genuine interest in the relationship, providing value and staying connected over time. Whether it's through a thoughtful message, sharing a relevant article, or checking in periodically, following up is a key ingredient in the art of networking that can significantly impact your professional growth and opportunities.

NETWORKING FOR **INTROVERTS**

CHAPTER 18
WE'RE ALL IN THIS TOGETHER
–UBUNTU

The African concept of Ubuntu – "I am because we are" – profoundly influences my networking philosophy. We are all in this together and we are all connected!

Ubuntu emphasises communal relationships, interconnectedness and mutual support. In the context of networking, Ubuntu can reshape how people engage with each other professionally in several meaningful ways:

Emphasis on Relationship Building
Ubuntu prioritises the creation and nurturing of relationships over transactional interactions. Networking, under the influence of Ubuntu, becomes an avenue to build genuine connections, where the focus is on understanding and supporting each other's goals and challenges, rather than merely seeking immediate personal or professional gains.

"Ubuntu is the essence of being human. It speaks of the fact that my humanity is caught up, is inextricably bound up, in yours."

Desmond Tutu

Collaboration and Collective Success

Ubuntu encourages viewing success through a communal lens rather than as an individual achievement. In networking, this translates to a focus on how individuals can collaborate and contribute to the collective success of their community or industry. It fosters a mindset where sharing opportunities, knowledge and resources for the mutual benefit of all involved becomes a priority.

Empathy and Compassion

Ubuntu imbues networking with a sense of empathy and compassion, where each person's dignity and contribution is valued. This approach encourages a deeper understanding of others' perspectives and challenges, leading to more meaningful and supportive professional relationships.

Responsibility and Accountability

The philosophy of Ubuntu comes with a sense of responsibility towards others in your network. It promotes a culture where individuals feel accountable for the well-being and development of their colleagues and connections, fostering a supportive environment where people feel valued and empowered.

Mentorship and Development

Inspired by Ubuntu, networking can include a strong element of mentorship and personal development. There's a shared understanding that helping others grow and succeed contributes to the community's overall strength and well-being.

Holistic Approach

Finally, Ubuntu can encourage networking to take a more holistic approach, considering the personal, professional and societal implications of networking activities.

"A person with Ubuntu is open and available to others, affirming of others, and does not feel threatened that others are able and good."

Desmond Tutu

It encourages individuals to think about how their professional lives intersect with their values and the impact they have on their community and society at large.

In essence, Ubuntu can profoundly enrich networking by fostering a sense of community, shared growth and mutual support. It encourages individuals to approach professional relationships with generosity, empathy and a deep sense of interconnectedness, transforming networking from a self-serving activity into a collaborative, community- building endeavor.

In one of my favourite Networking books, *Never Eat Alone*, Keith Ferrazi says there has never been abetter time to reach out and connect.Society is increasingly being defined by interdependence and interconnectivity. The more everything becomes connected to everything and everyone else, the more we begin to depend on who and what we're connected with.

Rugged individualism may have ruled for most of the nineteenth and twentieth centuries. Community and alliances will rule in the twenty-first century. In the digital era where the Internet and technology have broken down geographical boundaries and connected hundreds of millions of people around the world, there's no reason to live and work in isolation. We've come to realise again, that success is not just contingent on cool technology and increased profits – it's dependent on who you know and how you work with them. We've rediscovered that the real key to profit is working well with other people.

"*Success in any field, but especially in business, is about working with people, not against them.*"

Helen Nicholson

PART 3
ACTION PLAN

My biggest wish for you as you complete Part Two "Master the Art of Networking" is to go out and take massive action.

Recap of Part 1 Brand You PTY LTD

1. Realise how the neuroscience of being an Introvert affects the way you respond to stimuli.
2. Package your brand in a mindful intentional way, taking into account your strengths.
3. Find out what your Personal Branding coffee stain is and fix it. You are more than your coffee stain!
4. Develop RQ (Relevancy Quotient) goals both personally and professionally every year, so your brand always grows and stays relevant.
5. You can't be Brave if you're not well!
6. The three top networking characteristics are:
    - Abundance – give generously to your network and give first
    - Curiosity – listen 60% of the time and talk 40% of the time.
    - Develop presence – work on your body language
7. Audit your network – get clarity on who your Mavens, Connectors and Personal Board of Directors are.
8. Become a master storyteller – practise, practise, practise.
9. At networking events – set yourself a target of two new people to meet at every event.

"No-one is coming! You are the one you've been waiting for!"

Helen Nicholson

- Break into a conversation of three
- Think of rowing to do great small talk: OAR – Observe, Ask and Reveal
- Remember and use the person's nameDeliver a great elevator pitch
- Follow-up

This is the networking skill-set for Introverts. Remember that it is a skill that CAN be learned and mastered, even by Introverts. It's also a contact sport - start with one-on-one connnections and grow from there. Be patient with yourself and don't give up. Learning a new skill takes time. Now go out there and make it happen!

I'm here as your Personal Branding and Networking cheerleader. If I can help in any way please don't hesitate to contact me at helen@tnco.co.za or check out the numerous networking resources at www.Helen-nicholson.com or the work our business does at: www.tnco.co.za.

Special thanks to my amazing TNCO (The Networking Company) design team, who went the extra mile producing this book:
Shina Soobramoney Gabriella de Gersigny Celeste Briel
Olivia Morrison

Editing:
Michelle Colyn
Colin Bryden

SOURCES AND BIBLIOGRAPHY

- "The Introvert Entrepreneur" by Beth Buelow
- "Quiet: The Power of Introverts in a World that Can't Stop Talking" by Susan Cain
- Medical Daily 2004- Research on the Neuroscience of Introverts and Extroverts
- "Standout" by Marcus Buckingham
- Gallup Strengths Finder – gallup.com/cliftonstrengths
- "Outliers" by Malcolm Gladwell
- "Re-inventing YOU" by Dorie Clark
- Niven Postma, CEO and founder of Niven Postma Inc and Harvard business Review Contributor- niven@nivenpostma.com
- Harvard Business Review article "How to build your Network" by Brian Uzzi and Shannon Dunlap- 2005
- Personal Boardroom Methodology- www.personalboardroom.com
- Harvard Business Review Article- "How leaders create and use networks" by Hermina Ibarra and Mark Lee Hunter- 2007
- Zoya Mabuto- Mokoditoa- CEO and founder of Zoya Speaks, zoya@zoyaspeaks.co.za
- Debbie Goodman, CEO and Founder of Jackhammer Executive Search, Debbie@jhammerglobal.com
- "How to work a room" by Susan Roane
- "Never Eat Alone" by Keith Ferrazi
- Joni Peddie, Behavioural Strategist, CEO Resilient People #BounceForward - joni@resilientpeople.co.za
- She Ignites- Online career development courses for talented women www.sheignites.co

SOURCES AND **BIBLIOGRAPHY**

Mindfulness:

How to Stay Sane in an Insane World.

Networking:

How to Get your Black Belt in Business Success

Both available on Amazon

Printed in Poland
by Amazon Fulfillment
Poland Sp. z o.o., Wrocław
02 November 2024

38c790a2-b565-4473-8496-56fcf7a4d0b0R01